BILL STATHOPOULOS

Cold Email Secrets

How to Build a $1M Business and Get Replies From Anyone Using Email

Contents

Preface

How Email Was Born

The first email ever sent was frustratingly banal for such a ground-breaking moment. It was something like "QWERTYIOP" – the first top row of letters on the keyboard! That was back in 1971, on a predecessor of the internet called ARPANET.

See, email existed before the modern internet or the "worldwide web." In fact, it wasn't until a few decades later that brands and marketers started to use email for commercial reasons and sell things through the Internet.

Seth Godin is said to have pioneered Email Marketing with Yoyodyne, one of the earliest companies to try and promote Internet startups via email. He still remembers when the dot-com people laughed at him.

Seth worked to educate brands on the importance of Email Marketing. He introduced the concept of Permission Marketing: reaching out only to people who want to hear from you and not wasting energy on those who don't know what you do.

"I'm not responsible for all the emails you get in your inbox," Seth once said. *"But*

the email you want to get? I'll take a little bit of credit for that."

But how do you and I fit into the story?

Chapter 1

Being a Connector

T here are three levels to building a successful business.

- Level one: The expert
- Level two: The team builder
- Level three: The connector

The first level is being an expert at your craft. That can be Marketing consulting, being a doctor, or working at a retail store. It doesn't matter.

You learn to set and achieve goals, which helps boost your self-esteem and build trust in yourself and your ability to make things happen. You also get to know the ins and outs of the industry as you develop your expertise.

This gives you the insights to establish a successful business by solving a specific problem or capitalizing on an opportunity you have identified.

The second level is learning to hire, train, manage, and work with other people to achieve your shared vision. You either learn this skill as a manager in-house or when assembling your first team as a founder.

The last level is building synergies with other brands – becoming proficient at connecting your vision with that of other people and businesses to achieve greater things together. If you haven't guessed already, email can play a huge role here.

Now, what does my own journey of being a connector look like?

A few years ago, I leveraged email to grow an E-commerce agency to $1M+ in revenue per year and expand to the U.S. market. That agency now works with clients like Fashion Nova, JCPenney, and 7 For All Mankind.

Using the expertise from those campaigns, I then built a Go-to-Market agency called SalesCaptain, which is now ranked top 5 in the UK. One of the first channels we excelled at was, of course, Cold Email.

Not only that but during my time at Ad World, I built the largest marketing lineup in history – securing speakers like Arianna Huffington, Scott Galloway, Tom Bilyeu, and the CMOs of Samsung and Mastercard. All without having big-name contacts or a huge network in the industry.

And how did I make all of that happen? Simply by applying the principles I share with you in this book.

It was not a straightforward journey, but it was totally worth the price. Looking back, that was my test to enter level three of building a successful business.

Learning to connect with others to achieve greater outcomes together than we would have ever been able to achieve as individuals. And this brings us to today.

I wrote this book to help other founders and businesses achieve some of the success my team and I have had with Cold Email. To learn how to connect with others without being perceived as spammers. And to share the processes and strategies for making Cold Email work.

So, let's get started!

Chapter 2

Why Email Still Rocks

Many years have passed since the introduction of email into our lives, bringing changes like the introduction of spam filters, the use of smartphones to open emails, and regulations like the GDPR. One thing remains the same, though. Everyone still owns an email address. And for most of us on the internet, our email functions as our digital ID.

As more and more people across the world get online, they also get an email address. They might also use their phone number to communicate in some cases, using apps like WhatsApp and WeChat, but everyone still has an email address that they open at least once a day. And that's even more prevalent in the business world.

Traditional Email Marketing, using email to sell to consumers, can still be very effective, but making it work has become more challenging than ever. Marketers know that the number of consumers that open and click on their emails is different from what it used to be.

Cold Email, on the other hand, is still a promising channel. It is no different than a regular email – it consists of a subject line, email body, and signature. However, it is optimized for building relationships with people who don't know you.

A significant benefit of Cold Email is that finding someone's business email is straightforward. Most business emails follow a few specific patterns, that are set by each company's IT department.

Every email from the same company follows the same format. If you find one person's email, it becomes easy to guess the email addresses of the entire company. All you need is a first name, last name, and company name.

Therefore, once we decide we want to turn a company into our customer, we can identify the people within that company we want to target and then simply click a button to get their email addresses.

Our target customers are professionals that communicate with other people, like their partners and suppliers, through email as well. That means they have to check their email inbox at least once a day.

Whether once every few days or weekly, we know that sending an email will enable us to get the attention of our recipient.

What about those that have personal assistants or other team members monitoring and filtering their email? Even if we can't reach our target customers directly, there are still ways to go around the gatekeepers and start a conversation about our products and services.

Email is an open protocol. It cannot be regulated by one specific company or email provider. This makes it a foundational channel for communication. Not only for this decade but the foreseeable future, as it's the only digital communication standard that works across businesses, countries, and markets.

If you have a proven business offering – meaning a service or product that solves specific market needs – then Cold Email can be a direct, profitable sales channel for your business to leverage.

Chapter 3

Cold Email Use Cases

C old Email is a great sales and networking channel. Almost every company out there is using it – from global players like Microsoft, Uber, and Airbnb to startups, companies with lean budgets, and companies looking to grow in new markets.

What are some of the use cases?

Recruiting Top Talent

If you're in the HR space, you can use Cold Email to recruit qualified people for open roles in your business – instead of having to wait for the right candidate to discover and apply to your job posting.

Getting PR and Media Coverage

You can use Cold Email to get free PR and media coverage. Make a list of journalists from publications that cover topics relevant to your industry, and reach out with a recent update in your business or a groundbreaking new development.

Onboarding SaaS Users

Another application is as an in-house tool when onboarding new users to your SaaS or digital platform. Your product success representatives and onboarding specialists can reach out to new users, offer them a call with an account executive, and help them have a successful onboarding experience.

Partnerships

Another use case can be partnerships. You can use email to reach out to companies relevant to yours but not competitors that have access to the same audience you seek to target. For example, what if Uber reached out to Airbnb for a collaboration to provide discounted transportation between the airport and the Airbnb a traveler has booked for their trip?

Airbnb provides its users with convenience and potentially gains a new income stream. Whilst Uber gets access to an entire network of travelers, it can now convert into ride-sharing customers. Pretty cool, right?

Getting Featured in Events

Email can also be a way to get featured in events or invite people to create content with you, whether you're hosting a conference or looking to start your podcast.

During my time as the Director of Strategy and Content for Ad World, I used Cold Email to recruit speakers and build the world's largest advertising conference.

Applying the principles in this book, I was able to get replies from people like Satya Nadella (Microsoft CEO), Arianna Huffington's team, Sir Richard Branson, Amazon's leadership team, Apple's PR team, the global CMOs of Mastercard, Pepsi, and Samsung, and hundreds more companies and influencers I never thought I could reach.

Getting a response doesn't always mean it's a 'yes' or 'no' to your request. Cold Email can be a success even if the recipient forwards your email to the appropriate department within the company, signaling that it's not spam and that someone needs to look into it further.

For instance, when I emailed Satya Nadella to speak at Ad World, he didn't respond to me directly. He or his team read my email and forwarded it to Microsoft's PR team. Then the PR team responded to me, and we started discussing the speaking opportunity. If you ask me, that's still a win!

Building a Sales Pipeline

Lastly, you can use Cold Email for sales and business development. This is where it really shines, as it can be an essential driver of new revenue for your business.

You can always use it to attract new employees and then attribute the growth in your revenue to the new hire, but what's even more impactful is using Cold Email to build your sales pipeline. To generate new leads and deals for your company.

There are many more use cases and opportunities with Cold Email, but I hope by now you have an idea of what's possible. Later in the book, I'll walk you through proven Cold Email templates you can leverage for each use case to succeed with Cold Email.

Chapter 4

Who is Cold Email for

D*oes Cold Email work for everyone?*

Just like peanut butter and jelly isn't for everyone, neither is Cold Email. When it comes to sales, in particular, Cold Email works best for specific kinds of businesses and offerings.

The types of businesses that can benefit most are B2B service businesses and high-ticket software products.

Let's break this down a bit. For a company to make the most out of Cold Email for sales, they have to be a B2B company. This means they need to be selling to other companies.

They also have to be a service business or a software business, although that's not absolute. It could be a marketing agency, product agency, design agency, web development agency, or even a consulting firm. It can also be a software business like a digital product, app, or SaaS solution.

These services and products also need to be high-ticket. For every company or target client you reach out to, whatever you're selling should be worth at least $10,000 a year. Whether that's the price of your software for 100 users or a contract to build a website.

'Why $10k specifically?' I hear you ask. Well, this number is the result of a lot of experimentation, and it's based on the economics of Cold Email.

When you're doing media buying – whether that's Facebook ads, LinkedIn ads, or good old billboard ads – you need to have a specific ad budget. You have to pay the advertising network or the company that installs billboards to show your banner and deliver the traffic.

With Cold Email, you don't have any ad-related costs. What you do have is human-related costs. To run and scale Cold Email campaigns – also known as Outbound Sales – you need people.

And not just any old people, no. You need a specialized team, whether that's for building lists of prospects or for reaching out and following up on the leads you generate.

Therefore, you have to build your team and also pay for the cost of the tools that are required. We'll look into the breakdown of the team members and software you need later, but for it to make sense financially, the deals you're generating with Cold Email should be worth at least $10,000 a year.

Now, it's not the end of the world if you're a business with an average revenue per user or target client slightly lower than that mark. However, the absolute sweet spot is between $10K - $100K per year. Anything above that, and we're talking about enterprise sales, which is an entirely different game.

If the revenue per client is between $10K - $100K, you can automate part of the sales process and use digital tools to become efficient. For deals closer to $100K and above, you can use Business Development Reps (BDRs) to generate prospect lists and reach out manually. *Stick around, and I'll walk you through all of this.*

To recap, Cold Email can be a perfect channel for sales. If you use the right Cold Email approach based on your business models and the deal sizes we discussed above, it can be an absolute gold mine.

Chapter 5

Ads vs. Cold Email

L ong story short, using Cold Email to generate sales deals can be even more effective than Facebook ads when done right.

That's especially true if your business is in a stage where you're trying to validate whether there's a market willing to pay for your product or service. Or if you're looking to define the best messaging for a new market.

In terms of what it takes to generate a lead – someone interested in your products and services – Cold Email can have a lower Cost per Lead (CPL) than Facebook.

An average CPL for Facebook ads is between $25 and $100 – if you're lucky. LinkedIn is even more expensive. The cost per lead can go all the way up to $200 - $450, simply due to the nature of and costs of the platform.

Generating a lead when what's at stake is a $10K+ deal is not a small thing, right? Facebook and LinkedIn do understand that, and charge accordingly.

Running lead generation ad campaigns for B2C products is a much easier game.

Let's say you're running a B2C e-commerce store where the average product costs between $50 - $250. The lead costs much less to acquire for two main reasons:

- Each lead – or potential customer – is worth less in B2C
- The target audience with B2C products is much larger, and thus easier to find and target

If the revenue per deal is above $10K per year, as is the case with most B2B businesses, though, each lead is bound to cost more to generate. So if you're running ads to bring leads for a B2B business, you're looking at $200+ per qualified lead.

With Cold Email, the CPL can go all the way down to $20 - $25. As we've already discussed, the biggest cost is paying the team that is sending out emails. Let's assume we hire a qualified individual based in the Philippines – with good English language and digital skills – to send Cold Emails on our behalf. This role is called a Business Development Representatives (BDRs).

Your new BDR, with a little training, can cost between $500 - $700 a month. And they can generate between 20-50 appointments in a single month. Let's say the average is 20 appointments, which is still a good number. Each appointment now costs you $25 to book.

Even with a lower number of appointments per month, it's still a cost-effective way to generate leads.

So, when comparing the CPL of Cold Email vs. Advertising for B2B businesses, Cold Email is a clear winner. I'm not going to recommend it's the only channel you implement for your business. However, it should definitely be one of the first channels you invest in, especially if you don't already have massive brand awareness.

Chapter 6

The Opportunity with Cold Email

A t any given point in time, about 3% - 10% of any market is at the decision stage. This means that a certain percentage of the companies that fit your target client criteria are looking to buy services and products similar to yours within a timeframe of 1 - 3 months.

These are the prospects you always need to prioritize with your sales process, especially in the early stages of your business.

Why is this critical?

If you're just starting your business, or want to test out a new product, you don't want to spend time reaching out to people who might take 3 - 10 months to buy and need to be educated on the benefits of your solution.

It's the same with picking fruits from a tree. You want to start from the 'lowest-hanging fruit', which is easier to pick. How do we do that?

You could use targeted ads or, my favorite method, Cold Email. Here's why I prefer emails:

- It's quick and cost-effective to launch your campaigns
- It scales well without high additional costs
- Prospects can respond directly with specific feedback if they don't like your emails

Contrary to popular opinion – typically coming from email spammers – you don't need to email thousands of prospects each month. You can start small, refine your Cold Email and sales process, and gradually scale up as you succeed.

A good starting point is reaching out to around 2,000 prospects per month, which requires just one Business Development Representative (BDR) to work.

As your business grows, you can expand your reach and target new markets by adding more BDRs. The outreach process remains the same. Similar templates, similar tools, and the same messaging. Scaling Cold Email campaigns remains straightforward.

Another benefit of Cold Email is that it can help validate your business idea by providing crucial market feedback. Whether you're launching a new product or testing a startup concept.

Let's assume we use Facebook ads and Cold Email to understand the market's reaction to our product. With both these channels, you'll almost immediately begin to see results after you launch your campaigns.

At this stage, your primary goal is to get feedback from the market to validate your business assumptions. Sales will come as a side-effect if you do this step right.

However, what happens if your Facebook or LinkedIn ads are not working?

You get low click-through rates (people are not clicking your ads), a high cost per click (CPC), and low conversions regarding calls booked. Most people just ignore ads they don't resonate with. You're not getting any feedback as to why your messaging and targeting are not working. This is how people end up believing: *'Oh, Facebook ads don't work.'*

On the other end, if you mess up the targeting or the messaging with Cold Email, people are going to respond with direct, brutally honest, – sometimes hurtful – 'feedback'. This is what happened with one of my first Cold Email campaigns...

It went so bad; we did so many things wrong that people kept replying:

- *'Please stop emailing us.'*
- *'I never asked for this.'*
- *'This is not relevant to us at all.'*
- *'Stop the spam.'*

From the first week of running the campaign, the feedback was there. Email is such a personal channel that if you mess it up, you're going to know quite fast. This gives it a competitive edge over running advertising campaigns for market validation.

What happened with my campaign, you ask?

We kept iterating, and over time the results improved dramatically, making it one of our first Cold Email case studies. Let me now show you what success looks like with Cold Email.

Chapter 7

The Gold KPIs of Cold Email

W *hat does it look like to be successful with Cold Email?*

We've sent out more than 100,000 emails to prospects across different industries, markets and countries so far. And we've also built over a hundred campaigns for clients.

Over time, we've been able to define what we call the Gold KPIs of Cold Email.

The Gold KPIs are specific benchmarks that indicate your campaigns are performing well. If your campaigns are performing below these benchmarks, it means you need to be optimizing your targeting, message, landing page or call to action.

Goes without saying that these KPIs are going to differ based on the audience you're reaching out to. Here are the main variables that affect them:

- **Company size:** small businesses vs. enterprises

- **Region or country:** where your prospects are located in
- **Industry:** some industries prefer email and LinkedIn, while others – like plumbers or electricians – rely on their phones more
- **Role in the organization:** decision-makers and senior executives vs. managers and users are going to have different reply rates

So let's dive into the Gold KPIs of Cold Email.

- **Open Rate:** how many people opened your emails
- **Click-through rate (CTR):** how many people clicked on the links within your email
- **Reply rate:** how many people responded to your emails
- **Lead Rate:** how many meetings and positive replies you were able to generate from your sequence

The first thing you need to measure is your **Open Rate.** *How many people open my emails?*

A good open rate is around 60% - 70% when targeting small businesses with up to 100 - 200 employees. The open rate gets a bit lower if you're reaching out to enterprises, however, it shouldn't fall below 40%.

A low open rate means one of three things:

- Your list is not clean enough. You're sending emails to people and they're not getting delivered or opened.
- You're landing on the spam folder. Most Cold Email tools will let you know if this is the case, and help you fix this.
- You're reaching out to more decision-makers than end users. These

people just don't open their emails as much.

The second KPI is the **Clickthrough Rate**. *How many people as a percentage click through on the links you have on your email?*

A click-through rate of 5% - 10% is considered quite good.

The third KPI is the **Reply Rate**. *How many people are responding?*

This includes both positive and negative replies. It can be on average around 7 - 10%. It's one of the key indicators that there's interest in our campaigns, and one of the most important KPIs overall.

Some industries have increased reply rates and some segments have decreased reply rates. People in IT, for example, will have lower reply rates than other functions within the business. Marketing prospects might have increased reply rates. Similarly for people working in Customer Support, as they're always on top of their inbox.

Another important metric is the **Lead Rate**. We can also call these the 'conversions' of our campaign. *These are the people who replied positively, booked a sales call, started a free trial, or performed the conversion event we have set for our campaign.*

This is what a positive response looks like:

- *'I'm interested!'*
- *'What does your pricing look like?'*
- *'Do you have any case studies?'*
- *'Do you have any playbooks?'*
- *'Can I get a free trial'*

- *'Do you offer any personalized demos?'*

A good Lead Rate is between 0.5% - 2%. Whether prospects end up booking a call or just reply positively to one of your emails, we report them the same. Always keeping in mind that we have to follow up with the prospect in both cases.

Now that we've gone through each of the Gold KPIs, let's see what they would look like when running a campaign. Let's assume we're reaching out to 2,000 prospects in the period of one month.

Here's what it would get us:

Funnel Breakdown		Gold KPIs
Emails Opened	1200	Open Rate: 60-70%
Link Clicks	100	CTR: 5-10%
Replies	140	Reply Rate: 7-10%
Leads	10	Lead Rate 0.5-2%

These might not be the results your campaign receives with the first iteration. That's okay. The goal is to keep refining your targeting and your messaging. The more you do that, the more your Reply Rate is going to increase. Until you eventually get to 10+ leads per month.

We've run campaigns where the Reply Rate is above 30%. We were able to pull it off by reaching out to a really small group of people, 300 leads, and having really personalized messaging for each prospect.

That's not what the average Cold Email campaign looks like, though.

So let's fix that.

HOMEWORK: *Copy the Cold Email funnel breakdown on a Google Sheet and map out how many prospects you will need every month to hit your sales and lead generation goals.*

Chapter 8

What Happens If You Mess Up

ne of the main issues of doing Cold Email is the consequences of doing it wrong. Here are some examples of ways in which Cold Email can go wrong:

- Receiving harsh feedback
- Your email accounts get blocked
- Getting your domain blacklisted
- Creating a bad reputation for your business
- You might get reported for spamming
- You become demoralized

Receiving Harsh Feedback

You're most likely not creating personalized emails for each of your target audiences. In this case, you get immediate, harsh feedback. I can tell you that it didn't feel great to read responses calling my campaign spam. Over time, as you optimize your campaigns, the amount of bad feedback you receive eventually decreases.

Unlike Content Marketing and SEO, where the results might come three or four months later, with Cold Email there are immediate benefits. Literally, when you launch a new campaign, you can have see the opens and clicks, and you'll receive responses as well. This allows you to judge the performance of your campaigns much faster, compared to other channels.

My first Cold Email campaign was a big fluke. We ended up getting so many negative responses. But it was also a good way to get feedback on our process. People were saying that we were messaging them too frequently, so we increased the number of days before a follow-up.

In fact, we channeled every bit of feedback gathered into improving our next campaigns.

Your Email Accounts Get Blocked

With Facebook, Google, and LinkedIn ads, if people don't resonate with your message, the worst they can do is not click on the ad. They might even drop a negative comment. *Ooopsie, but still manageable.*

However, with Cold Email, if prospects don't resonate with your message, they can really easily mark your email as spam. Eventually, getting your email account blocked.

That's why it's really important to always be on the safe side and practice what we call the 'Mom Rule' of email. Treating your prospects like you would treat your mum. *You wouldn't spam your mom, right? Most of us, at least....*

If an email account is marked as spam, many of your emails end up in the spam folder, and eventually, that account gets blocked. Now you can't use them and need to wait 3 - 4 weeks to get them back into action or warm up new accounts, which takes the same time.

Just imagine if five of your accounts got marked as spam within the same month. Your campaigns would be hammered.

The price you pay if you don't follow good practices, and have a really good level of personalization is quite high. Even if you have backup accounts in place, that would still cost a lot to maintain. *Which leads us to the next point..*

Getting Your Domain Blacklisted

An immediate consequence of your emails being flagged as spam over and over again, is that your domain will end up getting blacklisted. This makes it really hard to continue running Cold Email campaigns without interruption.

When you have a domain name, let's say 'salescaptain.io', this domain name has a reputation. There are services online, whose purpose is to determine who's spamming on the internet. They do that by analyzing data and emails from providers like Gmail, Outlook, and Yahoo! Mail.

If you're caught spamming, your domain gets a bad reputation.

There's a good chance that, if your domain gets blacklisted, any emails from your domain will end up in the spam folder as well. This is a big issue as it's hard to recover a domain once it has been blacklisted.

Creating Bad Reputation for Your Business

A dangerous consequence, especially for established companies, is hurting your brand reputation.

Let's imagine a scenario.

You're a software company that's just launched a new product - a customer support tool for e-commerce businesses, similar to Gorgias.

You're eager to promote your product and bring in demos, so you reach out to a whopping 10,000 Shopify store owners at once, without having tested your campaign.

What if your messaging is off? You create a wave of negative sentiment within your target companies. They'll most likely be like, 'Hey, this company is spamming us.', or 'Oh, they've spammed us too.'

This backlash can damage your brand's reputation. It's especially harmful for larger, well-known brands. The risk is smaller for startups, but you still want your outreach to be carefully planned and personalized.

You Might Get Reported for Spamming

There is always the case you might get reported to the Better Business Bureau (BBB) for spamming – or an equivalent organization if you're not in the US.

These organizations are responsible for issuing fines to companies that send mass spam communications, so you don't want to end up in the list of companies they're looking into.

Unlike what some people might think, GDPR is not an issue here. GDPR is the data regulation that applies within the European Union when reaching out to European citizens, but it applies mostly to B2C communications.

GDPR doesn't apply if you're reaching out to a professional from a specific company, at their company email address for business development reasons. Provided of course that your message is personalized.

This is important to distinguish because a lot of people have doubts about whether Cold Email is even legal to do if you're in the EU.

You Become Demoralized

What happens if you manage to get a good open rate or click-through rate, but the campaign fails to materialize in terms of results?

You don't get conversions, replies, or sales. You get disappointed. Blame Cold Email. Blame this book. You eventually give up. *That's not what we want.*

During the optimization chapter, I'll show you exactly how to improve your Cold Email campaigns so they can generate a steady stream of leads every month.

Chapter 9

The Sales Mindset

One of the best skills you can learn in life is how to sell. Cold Email is one of the foundational channels you can use to sell online.

It's a tough skill to learn and practice because until you get your messaging right, you're going to receive a lot of negative responses. However, it can also be one of the most rewarding skills.

If the offer, messaging, and audience are aligned, Cold Email can bring an immediate boost to your business – *and there's nothing more rewarding than that.*

I like to think of the sales mindset as being like that of a hound. You have to keep a specific target in mind, be able to identify and lock your target in – and then not let go until you have achieved your goal.

The rule of thumb for sales, and also for cold email, which is a close analogy, is it takes 10 'no's to get to one 'yes.' That's a lot of unresponsive prospects and negative responses to get to someone saying, 'Yes, I'm interested in a meeting.'

This means you have to be persistent, especially if you're the one sending all the emails out manually. This is why having a hound mentality matters.

You might want to target someone from Microsoft to demo your product or service. To get a positive response, you might have to reach out to three or four people within Microsoft, throughout two campaigns and over six months.

You have to remain laser-focused in the meantime. Going after additional prospects from each company if the first prospect doesn't respond. Ideally, you start from as high in the company's hierarchy as it makes sense and work your way down.

I know, it's a lot of effort – but boy, are the results worth it.

Adopt the mindset of: *'I have to have Microsoft as a client because they align with our ideal customer profile.'*

And if you keep pushing forward, eventually you're going to make it. Every time you get a 'no', you can either view it as a failure or you can view it as one more step towards a 'yes'. That's the sales mindset.

Truth is, there's always someone in need of your product or services. Selling is the act of reaching out to them. Nothing else.

Being patient enough to go through the nine people who are gonna say no, so you can get to the one person who's at the right moment, at the right time, in the right buying stage, and is going to buy from you.

It's a positive and value-adding activity that contributes to society. As long as you're not trying to scam people, of course, or sell them things they don't need. This is not something I would ever advocate for.

One key element here is we also wanna feel good about ourselves when selling. Treating others the way we would want to be treated. This way you increase your chances of sticking with Cold Email long enough until you start seeing results.

Then it becomes much, much easier. The moment positive responses start coming in, everything clicks. In a nutshell, the mindset you need to have in order to be successful with Cold Email is this:

'There's someone out there, in need of my product or my service. I have to be specific about who they are, and I need to keep working until I've found that person.'

So, channel your inner hound: sniff out the right trail with patience and persistence, and you'll eventually find the 'yes' hiding in the forest of 'no's.

Chapter 10

Create a Winning Offer

The Problems of a Bad Offer

P eople think that Cold Email starts from writing the copy for a campaign, setting up the sequence, building a contact list, and clicking 'Send'. This couldn't be further from the truth.

Cold Email is just another user acquisition and sales channel that you can leverage to build your business. However, because of the nature of the channel, if your offer is not on point, your message will be off, and this increases your chances of being marked as spam significantly.

This is not really an issue when running paid ads campaigns. A bad offer or messaging just means fewer clicks and conversions, and probably a wasted ad budget.

There are no meetings, there are no leads. There's nothing. So you turn the campaigns off. It's really straightforward. Same with Content Marketing and SEO.

You perform the activity. It's not working out. You are not ranking on Google. You're not getting any backlinks. People are not sharing your content. You get demotivated and you think that this doesn't make sense. You want to stop. *I get it.*

However, Cold Emails and Outbound Sales force you to nail your message and Product/Market fit. Otherwise, you risk getting demoralized fast. You never get any positive replies. Or if you do get some, it might be either from an unqualified lead or someone who is not your ideal client. And you abandon the channel.

Having said that, if you've been able to achieve good performance on other performance marketing channels, like paid ads, you should be able to scale your Cold Email campaigns and achieve similar results from that channel

A good combination of offer, messaging, and audience that works on one channel can be adapted to work for Cold Email, and vice versa.

Pitch an Offer, Not a Service

So what are some offer examples, and how can an offer be good or bad? It has to do with the type of business you're reaching out to. And also with what you're asking, what you're providing, and how much you're charging for it.

So let's go through the basic offer components:

- Target audience
- Dream outcome
- The audience's problems

- Identifying solutions for each problem

The first one is the **target audience**. The audience is always the first thing we need to be clear about. Defining what kind of people or companies it consists of, and what kind of characteristics this audience shares so we can identify and target them.

The second one is the **dream outcome**. What is the big goal that this specific audience is aiming to achieve? It's all about making their dream outcome effortless. Reducing the amount of time that it takes to see the outcome, making it realistic and specific.

Let's say my dream goal is to generate 1,000 leads a month from my website – what kind of problems would I face? And what kind of solutions would I need to achieve my goal?

There are different **problems** along the way and different micro-goals you need to achieve.

For example, if you want to generate 1,000 leads, you need a landing page for the leads to visit and convert. You need a form on that landing page. And the page needs to be optimized for conversions. Then you need someone to drive traffic to the landing page so that you can convert it into leads.

So the offer consists of picking a specific audience, selecting a dream outcome, then defining their problems and identifying the right solutions.

Now let's look into **solutions** for our problem.

Let's go back to our Marketer from the previous example, who needs to build a landing page and run ads to generate leads. What can you offer as a business to help them? Would you offer them a landing page builder, a course on how to build a landing page and run ads, or a web development service?

Time to put everything together.

The components of the offer are essentially all the solutions that are required to solve the problem. So your offer, with its different components, should look like this:

- Offer component #1: We'll build your landing page
- Offer component #2: We'll optimize the landing page so that it converts better
- Offer component #3: We'll run ads targeted to the landing page, etc.

There are additional components to a good offer, like bonuses and a guarantee, but simply putting together a solid solution can make your offer stand out.

Having specific offer components also allows you to test different offers and different variations of your offer until you find the one that works best for you.

Offer Examples

Let's look at a real-life example. Let's say you are a marketing agency and you want to offer a Paid Ads service. Here are some different offer examples, quite distinct from one another.

The first one is a **done-for-you service** or full implementation offer. The messaging and the position would be something like this:

'We'll run your ads for you. You don't have to do anything. We'll take over the entire thing. We'll build the creatives and landing page as well.'

The second one could be a **consulting and training offer**. Something like:

'We'll work with you on the strategy for the paid ads and then train you and your team on how to run the ads so you can be very effective.'

Another type of offer could be a **hiring and training offer**.

'Will he help you hire a rockstar media buyer, then train that person on the specifics of your business so that they can run, monitor and optimize the ads.'

Another element could be a **SaaS offering**, selling them software.

'We will give you access to our platform that generates ad creatives and automates your ad campaigns with a few clicks.'

Another one could be **offering a book** and saying:

'You want to learn how to run paid ads? Perfect. My new book will show you how to implement everything in the next 90 days.'

These different types of offers depend on the stage of your business, the types of companies you're reaching out to, your pricing model, and your team structure. Ultimately it comes down to your preferences as a founder and your strengths as a business.

Channel Not Working VS. Bad Offer

It's always important to remember that if your offer is not tested and fine-tuned, there's a good chance that Cold Email is not going to work. If your offer is working on one channel, it should also work with Cold Email.

What does it mean that Cold Email works for a specific offer?

It's quite specific.

The first step in achieving the Gold KPIs of Cold Email is having an open rate above 60%, a reply rate above 5% or above click-through rate of 5% and above, and a lead rate above 0.5%

If you hit the Gold KPIs, you should be getting positive results out of your campaigns. If you're not able to hit your Gold KPIs, you might have a bad offer, a message problem, or bad targeting.

So before killing your cold email campaigns, you should consider either fixing your offer or changing your messaging.

When you're marketing a new product or service, don't approach the market looking to sell. Aim to get feedback on your offer first. Approach your prospects and say, 'Let me show you what I have in mind, and I would appreciate any feedback you have.'

If you've nailed your offer and messaging, and people resonate with it, chances are they will be willing to buy from you. If you go to the market and they 'Need to think about it,' keep updating your offer and messaging, and then reach out again.

If you do that, I guarantee you that Cold Email will work. Your offer is going to get much better, and you're going to be able to reach product market fit and then be able to scale cold email as a channel.

HOMEWORK: *Review the offer examples, pick one for your business, and rewrite it to be crystal clear. Make sure you include all the offer components required to build a complete solution.*

Chapter 11

Build Your Ideal Customer Profile (ICP)

W hat's the #1 rule of marketing?

That's right - any form of non-personalized messaging or advertising is...

Yup - SPAM!

When you're watching an ad on TV that is not targeted to you, you instantly change the channel. Through something called *ad fatigue*, we have learned to tune out most ads we see on television or online unless they're targeted at us.

This explains why the clickthrough rate of ads on publisher websites is now around 0.03%. Even with Facebook ads, as people kept seeing ads repeatedly, the clickthrough rates dropped significantly – and conversions, too.

Let's cover some ways to ensure your cold emails don't suffer the same fate!

Having non-personalized messaging when sending cold emails means that you're not only classified as spam and irrelevant, but also you're really likely for your messages to be marked as spam.

In both the literal and metaphorical sense, a non-personalized cold email is spam. It's the one mistake you can't afford to do.

This is why the first actual step in building your messaging is defining the target persona that you're going to be reaching out to.

Within B2B Sales and Marketing, we have one really common term, which is the **Ideal Customer Profile (ICP).** Instead of saying target audience, we say ICP. When you're doing Cold Email, we typically recommend defining and targeting between 1 - 3 ICPs.

Similarly, when we're starting to go to market, we want to pick between 1 - 3 different audiences, distinct groups of companies with specific characteristics to target – as we don't know for sure which group is going to perform best.

Sales, as we know, is a dynamic process that evolves with time. We listen, we learn, we adjust. We start asking questions - How long does it take to close a deal? Which industries open their wallets wider for our products or sign on for larger deals?

This feedback, this real-world wisdom, helps us home in on our Ideal Customer Profiles (ICPs). Sure, we can—and will—add more ICPs as we grow, but starting with 3 well-defined ICPs allows us to focus and create more personalized campaigns.

You don't want to start with 10 ICPs, because each one requires a list of different prospects, different targeting, different messaging, different campaigns, and different analytics.

With every ICP you add, the complexity of your campaign increases significantly, as you have to do a lot more work to get the campaigns live.

How do we go about defining our ICPs?

Broadly speaking, there are three categories that we typically focus on and that can be used to define an ICP. These are firmographics, demographics, and psychographics.

Firmographics

When we select the targets for our outbound campaigns, we typically start by defining specific firmographics and identifying the companies that fit those criteria.

In a B2B context, this is one of the most valuable traits, as it helps you identify the companies to target. It can include everything from company size, HQ location (where they are located), funding rounds (have they raised money), team size, annual revenue (or other revenue figures), department size, and the industry.

Here are some of the firmographics characteristics:

- Location & geographies
- Industry
- Company size/employee count
- Revenue per year
- Technologies they use or invest in (e.g. Amazon AWS, Hubspot, Shopify Plus, etc.)
- Funding rounds

An example would be targeting automotive companies based in the US, which have between 50 and 100 employees or 500-1,000 employees.

Demographics

We then narrow our search from the companies down to the individual prospects and the professionals that you're looking to sell to. These characteristics are called **Demographics**, and include:

- Job Title
- Seniority
- Department
- Years of experience in the company or a role
- Company name
- Education
- Language

An example of demographics targeting would be:

'I want to target marketers based in Oklahoma City or New York City who are between the ages of 25 and 35 and who have ten years of experience, so they have been working the last ten years as marketers.'

Demographics only provide you details on who the professional is that you have in front of you and what traits they might have.

Psychographics

The last category, and the most important one for creating personalized copy, is psychographics.

Psychographics cover the emotional and mental traits of your audience. This is related to the people themselves – their goals, problems, fears, values, interests, habits, attitudes, beliefs, motivation, prioritization, and preferences.

Examples of psychographic characteristics could be:

- What have these people tried to do to solve the problem that you have identified that failed, that didn't work?
- What could make them worry that they're making the wrong choice?
- What alternatives are they looking into?
- What other products are they looking into?
- What results do they expect to achieve by purchasing your solution?
- Which features of competing companies, products, or services do your customers consider essential to make a purchase? What are their expectations for each feature?
- What did they do first when they decided to shop for a solution like the one you offer?
- Who's an influencer or media source they would look up to for business topics that would influence their decision to purchase?

In order to create a winning offer and messaging, we need to identify a specific problem that our target businesses and people face and then a solution to their problem. A dream outcome.

The problem might be company-wide. For example, a Marketer's problem could be they're not generating enough leads or lack a proven marketing process. However, you're not reaching out to a business. You're reaching out to the individual.

Therefore, you need to figure out how the larger problem impacts each individual within a company.

Psychographics is the most useful element for creating personalized email copy, as it allows you to tie the company's profile and needs with the individual's goals and produces copy that resonates with them. As a result, you end up closing the sale because people buy from people (who understand them), even in a B2B context.

Here's an example where we used psychographic data to close a sale:

You're trying to sell your cutting-edge email marketing software to a company. You've done your homework on the demographic data – the head of marketing, the CFO, and a few key players in the marketing team. But to truly connect and convince, you need to dive deeper and understand their psychographics.

You discover that the CFO has shown interest in AI and machine learning. Highlighting your software's AI-driven analytics and predictive capabilities in your email caught their attention. They forward your email to the CMO. The CMO reaches out to you and requests a demo of the AI features. Sold!

Targeting Enterprise Accounts

Are you only selling to one person per company?

When we sell to B2B companies, it's always important to have in mind the following roles:

- The user of the tool or solution
- The person responsible for deciding which tool the company is going to buy
- Who is approving the budget

In some cases, especially in smaller companies, the same individual is responsible for making the decision and approving the budget.

However, in larger firms or when selling an enterprise-level service, the approval chain expands. You may need the CFO or the head of marketing to greenlight the purchase, while the actual users could be the in-house engineers or marketing experts.

So, when you're crafting your Cold Email strategy targeting enterprise businesses, you need to identify the key decision-makers and the ones who hold the purse strings. Yes, the experts matter, but usually, they aren't your primary audience. They don't hold the decision-making power.

That's why you need to keep in mind the demographics of your target company. Identifying the decision maker, their boss, and the person right below them in the org chart. These are the people we want to reach out to.

Then, within each outreach cycle, including at least two to three prospects from the same account. Especially for larger companies.

At the end of the day, successful selling comes down to three key elements:

- Precision targeting: zeroing in on the businesses that fit your niche or

Ideal Customer Profile (ICP).

- People-spotting: identifying the change agent within the company, driven by the right motives and ready to shake things up.
- Persuasive positioning: crafting the perfect angle and tapping into the psychographic sweet spot that resonates with your prospects.

Nail these, and you're going to have a very easy job selling.

HOMEWORK: *Download the Targeting & ICP worksheet from coldemailsecrets .co/resources, pick 2-3 niches you want to target, and fill it out.*

Chapter 12

Selecting a High-Converting Audience

I s there a way to ensure we're reaching out to the right prospects?

Even if you've never done Cold Email, or if you've never sold to the same industry, you can be effective if you put in the time for proper market research.

Surveying Existing Clients

The first research exercise you can do is surveying existing clients. Looking into traits your existing clients potentially share:

- Is there a specific industry that stands out?
- Are they all members of a specific Facebook group?
- Are they from a specific city?
- Are they part of a specific industry?
- Are they part of a specific demographic group?

- What was the problem they described?
- Did they come from a conference?
- Did they come because of the specific content you put out?
- What made them come to you?
- What type of content brought them to you?
- What kind of language did they use to describe your service?

When surveying your clients, ask them this question: *'How would you describe us to your mother to someone who doesn't know what we do?'*

'How would you describe our service' is a really good way to get insights on the copywriting front and how to actually structure your message so that it makes sense when you're writing the copy to other people from that industry as well.

That's all well and good if you already have clients within that industry. What happens if you haven't reached out to that industry before? Or if you have a new industry in mind that you'd like to reach out to, but don't know if it would work?

Using Cold Email to Find An Industry

Well, you can still use Cold Email, but you have to use it in a different way initially. You have to go a step back and use Cold Email to get insights, gather market information, and do some research on the specific prospects that you're looking to target.

Taking even a month to do research should be enough. Just by reaching out to people, asking them what they think about your solution, and what kind of problem they have, you're starting conversations that could potentially lead to sales. Without actually doing any hard selling.

What does the messaging look like in this case? You can run campaigns requesting a research interview. It could be something like:

Hey {{first name}}, I need your help.

I'm putting together a report on professionals in the industry, and I wanted to get your input. I will not be attempting to sell you anything, guaranteed.

It'll be a 30-minute interview, and we publish our findings online.

You can choose to remain anonymous if you wish. A great way to get some free publicity, as well as to help contribute to your field.

Are you free tomorrow {{time / 10 am PST}}?

This is a sample message. You can personalize it based on the industry that you're reaching out to and the position of the prospects.

Aim to reach out to 50-100 individuals from within the industries that you want to target in a period of a month. Then analyze the results.

Looking at the response rates and the type of solutions prospects they're looking into, you can position yourself much better.

Where to Find Your First Prospects

If you haven't done any of that before, here's the recipe you can use:

1. Open up LinkedIn Sales Navigator and select a few company filters, or type in an industry name on the search bar.
2. See what kind of companies and professionals show up, and which of them have full profiles filled out.
3. Visit the profiles of a few prospects.
4. Have a look at what they're discussing and what kind of posts they engage with.
5. Congrats! You now have a better understanding of your ideal prospects, their problems, and their thought process.

Using Groups for Research

Another place for research would be using Facebook groups within your niche.

If you're targeting eCommerce owners, there are a ton of eCommerce-related groups, whether it's marketing, founders, or anything else. Same for the automotive industry, the fashion industry SaaS companies, and pretty much any industry out there.

Learn to become a 'native' in the groups and communities you're looking to target. It can serve you well and allow you to shorten the time it takes to write good copy for that niche.

Once you have joined a community, ask questions to get to know your prospects better:

- *'Hey guys, I'm thinking about launching this type of service. Is there a problem you have?'*

- *'How would you go about solving this problem?'*
- *'Do any of you have this problem?'*

To sum up, by doing some proper market research, you are essentially building your ammo – doing the preparatory steps required so that when you reach out, you'll have better chances of getting a response.

HOMEWORK: *Do your research online and try to identify 5-10 groups and communities your ideal customers are hanging out in. Don't forget to check LinkedIn Sales Navigator.*

Chapter 13

Audience Research

Before generating prospect lists at scale from a new niche or ICP, we need to get clear about the following elements:

- How feasible is it to generate leads from this niche (easy, medium, hard)?
- How many companies exist in this niche?
- How many leads can we generate per day?
- Should we be making any tweaks in our targeting and our ICP to be able to generate more leads per day (e.g., targeting companies with 50-500 employees instead of only 50-100 employees)?

We typically call this **Audience Research** and perform it right after we define a new ICP. This also helps us get an understanding of the TAM (Total Addressable Market) of the ICP we have defined.

Total Addressable Market (TAM) is an important metric because it represents the maximum potential revenue that our business could generate by selling its product or service to the entire market.

The formula to calculate the TAM for a specific niche is simple:

TAM = Total potential customers in that market X Annual Contract Value (ACV)

By objectively estimating a market's potential for growth, the TAM provides a useful benchmark for evaluating the business opportunity of selling to a specific market. It also gives us a good indication of how long we can continue generating leads and running campaigns targeting that market before we exhaust the addressable audience.

Chapter 14

Building Targeted Prospect Lists

T
he real prospecting journey unfolds here - transforming your ICP into prospect lists by tracking down every potential prospect. This chapter will show you how to turn abstract ideas into actual clients, taking you one step closer to your goals.

Welcome to the art of prospect hunting!

How would you do that?

Selecting a Data Source

The first step is selecting a source. The source you pick will depend on the type of leads or the type of industries you want to target.

If you want to target people based on **demographic or firmographic data** – the type of company, the industry, the job title, or how long a prospect has been in their current position – **LinkedIn Sales Navigator** is a great place to start.

You'll want to get access to Sales Navigator and not go with a free LinkedIn account. LinkedIn is more tolerant when you're paying for their service and they give you access to some more research.

If you're looking to sell to **local businesses**, you'll need lists of plumbers, photo studios, cinemas, gyms, or any other local business. These businesses may have many physical stores across regions and cities. **Google Maps** data can be invaluable for tracking them down.

For more tools recommendations, go to coldemailsecrets.co/tools for up-to-date tools.

There are also ways to target companies based on their **tech stack** or technographic data. Things like their CRM, the platform that their website is built on, their ad platforms, or their CMS. Companies using Hubspot or a specific CRM. Websites built WordPress and stores using Magento or Oracle.

All these elements allow you to fine-tune your messaging.

The presence of a Facebook pixel could suggest past or ongoing Facebook ad campaigns. An installed LinkedIn pixel might indicate that they're running or contemplating LinkedIn ads.

You can even get a list of your competitors' clients, provided they sell software that you add to your website. **BuildWith** is a good source of technographic data.

If you're looking to go after companies that have recently raised a funding round or are looking to raise, Crunchbase is the perfect database.

Another category that's really interesting is **Ecommerce and DTC stores**. There are so many companies selling to consumers online right now. However, Ecommerce is still a really generic target to go after.

You want to go after specific niches within Ecommerce. Fashion brands, automotive brands, or any other product line that you're interested in. You don't want to go after everyone because it's not going to be personalized enough.

You'll want to pick different types of stores within Ecommerce. Tools like **Storeleads** and **Brandnav** can help you do that,

The last data category, which is the most interesting for B2B high-ticket sales, is **intent data**. You can target companies based on the type of content their employees are reading or looking into.

There are data providers like **Bombora** that collect that data. And then give you access to lists of companies looking for content and solutions similar to yours.

An example could be that someone from the Microsoft London office is looking at content related to purchasing a new CRM.

You can go to coldemailsecrets.co/resources to get a list of the intent data categories you can target.

List Building Framework

After we've identified the sources, let's go through the process of building an actual prospect list. Most data sources will give you a list of companies that fit your targeting criteria.

For every company, that includes the following details:

- Domain
- Company name
- Industry
- Number of employees
- Additional data (revenue, funding, etc.)

Everything is related to the account. So you pick a source, and you get a list of companies. From those companies, you want to find the decision-makers.

We know which job titles and departments work for us based on our ICP criteria. For larger companies, you want 3 - 4 people, and for small companies, you need 1 - 2 people.

Then you want to find the email addresses of those people. There's an entire list of tools that do just that. From Apollo all the way to ZoomInfo.

The reason this part is so easy is that most corporate email addresses or most business-similar addresses follow a few specific formats, as we've already discussed.

It's typically one of these combinations:

- firstname.lastname@company.com
- f.lastname@company.com
- lastname.f@company.com
- f@company.com

Verifying one email from a company, allows you to pinpoint how the company structures the email for each one of their employees.

You only need a first name, last name, and company name, and 9/10 times you can actually find an email address.

Once you have an email address, there are additional tools that verify if the email addresses you got is actually correct or not. This step sounds mundane, but you shouldn't skip it.

Just because you found an email address online, it doesn't mean that the email works, that it's still deliverable.

You need to verify it ideally using two different email verification tools, so when you're sending out your emails, you don't get a lot of emails not being able to be deliverable. That's called a bounce, and a high bounce rate is a signal that there's spamming going on. You definitely want to avoid that.

You can go to coldemailsecrets.io/tools for an up-to-date list of email finding and email verification tools.

And there you have it, my friend!

The science of building a robust prospect list. It's like playing detective, piecing together information to form a clear picture. The thrill when you correctly guess an email format? Priceless.

It's all part of the game, and trust me; it's a game worth playing.

HOMEWORK: *Update the Targeting & ICP worksheet with targeted criteria that match your target niches. Then, download the Audience Research report template from coldemailsecrets.co/resources and fill it out for the same niches.*

Chapter 15

Setting Up Your Inbox

You have your list of prospects at hand, and feeling ready to launch the campaigns. What's the next step? It's time to set up your email inboxes.

Buy a New Domain

The first step is buying a new domain. I know this might sound counterintuitive, but you don't want to do your outreach from the main domain of your business.

There is always the case that people might report your emails as spam, and get your entire domain blacklisted. It's rare, but still it's not a risk worth taking.

Most companies that do Cold Email buy a few domains similar to their main domain. Then set up new email accounts from those domains to run their campaigns.

Let's say your business is Microsoft and your main domain is microsoft.com. You might buy microsoft.io or microsoft.co. You can even get microsoft.co.uk if you're targeting companies based in the UK.

For every domain you buy, you want to create new inboxes. My recommendation is to create a maximum of three email accounts per domain.

This way you don't have too many email addresses sending out emails that can be marked as spam from the same domain.

In case something goes wrong and one domain gets blacklisted, you can still have the backup domain and accounts for your campaigns.

Determine the Outreach Personas

The next question to answer internally is whether you're going to use a persona versus a real person from the business to send out the emails on your behalf.

In most cases, I would recommend using a real person from your business. It looks and feels much more real, and you can also add links to their LinkedIn and Twitter profiles in the email signature.

Redirect the New Domains

We now need to redirect the new domains that we just bought.

For instance, if your main domain is salescaptain.io, and you start using salescaptain.co for your campaigns, you want the new domain to redirect people back to your main website.

This way, if someone visits that domain – and there's a high chance this is going to be the case – they are redirected to the main website.

In our first Cold Email campaign, once we started scaling and using more domains for outreach, our response rate dropped suddenly. We were wondering why that was until a prospect emailed us saying 'Hey guys, your website is blank'. That's when – and how – we figured we need to be redirecting our new domains. *The hard way.*

Forward Incoming Emails

Besides a redirection, you want to forward the emails that are coming into your new inboxes in your primary sales inbox.

What we typically do in this case is set up a group email address. Most email providers have this option. You set up a group email, which can look something like sales@company.com. For any emails coming to your inboxes, you forward them to your group address.

This becomes the one central address to manage everything, like a hub for your sales communications.

You then add any members of your sales team that need to be receiving those incoming emails to the group email. That could be your BDRs, your Sales Manager, and the person in charge of classifying and responding to incoming emails.

As you scale your outreach and add more than ten different inboxes, you don't want to be logging into every inbox every day. A group email allows you to have one central inbox.

Before we're able to send out any cold emails, we need to authenticate our sending domains with our new Cold Email tool. This happens once for every domain and includes setting up your SPF, DKIM, and DMARC records.

You can do a quick Google search on 'how to set up an SPF record and DMARC record'. Based on your email provider and domain host, you'll find specific instructions to add to your domain management platform (think Cloudflare, GoDaddy, etc.).

Determine How Many Accounts You Need

The next item on the list is figuring out how many email accounts you need. Start by creating 3-4 accounts for each domain you buy. Each of these accounts can safely send 50-80 emails per day.

If you're sending out emails 20 days per month, this means each account can reach approximately 1,000 prospects monthly.

If you use a Google Workspace email account, Google says you can send upwards of 200 emails a day, but I would recommend staying away from this limit, as it makes it easier for your inbox to get blacklisted.

Let's say your domain is salescaptain.io. Your email can have variations of your name, like bill@salescaptain.io, bill.s@salescaptain.io, and bill.stathi@salescaptain.io. You use the same naming convention across different domains.

Before figuring this out, and because we wanted to scale our outreach for one of my clients fast, we bought one new domain and set up 10 Google email accounts. Within a week of going live, with campaigns, all of our domains were blocked. *That set us back 3 weeks with our outreach, don't repeat our mistake!*

Use a Paid Email Provider

Another recommendation I would give is using is a paid email account. I've been asked: *'I've been using a free Gmail or Zoho mail account. Is that okay?'*

That's a no-go for multiple reasons. You can't have custom link tracking, which, if you're using links within your email might harm your deliverability. And you also appear really unprofessional.

Picture this: you're all set for a high-stakes poker game, and just when you're about to make your move, you pull out...a handful of Monopoly money. That's what it feels like when you're trying to spark high-value conversations via cold email using a free Gmail account. *It's a big no-no!*

Pick a Cold Email Tool

When it comes to your email-sending tool, you want to pick one that's designed for Cold Email.

People often ask me: *'Is it okay to use Hubspot or MailChimp to send my cold emails? I want to keep all my prospects in one place.'* The answer is 'no'. Cold Email is not the same as regular Email Marketing. So you can't use the same tools.

When it comes to 'keeping all your prospects in one place', trust me, you don't want 5,000 prospects per month to be added to your CRM – as would be the case if you're using Hubspot. Not to mention that Cold Email is against Hubspot's terms of use. *Not surprising, I know!*

Create Consistent Profiles

Once your email inboxes are live, you need to set up your profile for each one and keep it consistent.

What do I mean by that?

You are to make sure your Outlook or Google email includes a full name, a photo, phone number, and any other personal details that the email provider allows you to add.

When you're sending out an email, the first thing the recipient is going to see is your first name, your last name, the subject line, and maybe your profile picture. These elements can't be missing from your profile.

I would also recommend creating an account with Gravatar (that's gravatar.com) and uploading the profile picture there. Gravatar is a service that allows you to add a profile picture to any email address you own. It also makes certain spam filters trust you a bit more.

Sending Plain Text Emails

Any emails you send with your outreach accounts should be plain text emails. Avoid including media files like images, gifts, or attachments.

You can use maybe one image or one gift as a follow-up to your sequence, but just make sure it's one image. Never include attachments in your sequence. Most tools don't even allow you to add attachments, as they increase your risk of going into the spam folder.

For the same reason, don't include multiple links in your emails. Each link you add increases your chances of being marked as a spammer. It and also make it less likely that the person is going to respond to your message.

At this point, if you're wondering how many links your email should have, the answer is a maximum of 2-3 links. Remember that if you add a phone number or your website in your signature, these also count as links.

Include an Unsubscribe Link

I can't emphasize enough how important it is to Include an unsubscribe link or a clear way for people to unsubscribe from every email. This can be a line like: 'If you don't want to hear from me, just reply with 'stop''. Feel free to be creative here.

From tests we run, we figured out that there's a high chance that if you're reaching out to a Microsoft 365 email account, and none from your domain has ever emailed your prospects' domain, your cold emails will go to the spam folder automatically. Unless your emails include an unsubscribe link.

We had one campaign targeting enterprises that had a terribly low Open Rate and Reply rate. It took a while to realize that: a) most enterprises use Microsoft 365, b) because we didn't have unsubscribe links, our emails were going to spam.

Respect the Sending Limits

Now, it goes without saying that you need to respect the sending limits of the email provider you use. Part of being a good fellow is sending out personalized emails to the world. This means you can't really go super high in terms of volume. *It's a recipe for spam and negative replies.*

Stick to sending 50 - 80 emails per day, and create more email accounts if you need to be reaching out to more prospects than you currently are.

Unlike fruit, with Cold Email, the older the email account, the better it is in terms of its reputation and how many emails you can send from that account provided. Provided of course that you've been using the account to send out emails to people on a regular basis.

Determine Your Sending Schedule

Lastly, you want to send emails during specific days and hours of the week. In most cases, this means work hours for the country you're targeting.

You can experiment with whether sending out emails at the beginning the middle or the end of the workday helps increase your Open Rate and Reply Rate. Always tying that to your user's time zone.

If you have one campaign targeting prospects from the US, you should send your emails 9 am Pacific time so you can cover the entire continent. If you're reaching out to prospects in Europe, you can choose London time (GMT), to make sure that everyone is awake when they receive your emails.

In wrapping up, setting up your email for cold outreach includes a series of strategic steps. Not all fun, but necessary. Once you've implemented this process for a few domains, it should become second nature.

Keep refining, and keep learning. After all, your next big opportunity might be just an email away.

HOMEWORK: *Download the Outbound Tech Setup from coldemailsecrets .co/resources and fill it out. It will help you determine which domain to use, how many accounts you need, and all the technical parts of Cold Email.*

Chapter 16

Warming Up Your Inbox

One of the things that makes Cold Email so effective, is that it allows you to get into the user's inbox, and skip the 'Promotions' tab. The reason we use specific tools to send out cold emails is they allow us to do just that.

Without getting too technical, most Email Marketing makes it easy for email providers like Google and Outlook to identify and classify your emails as marketing emails, sending them to the Promotions tab.

To reach the primary tab you need a good email sender reputation for your email account. Your accounts don't have any reputation in the beginning – unless you're using old email accounts – so you have to build it.

How do you build a good email reputation?

You use specialized tools that send and reply to emails on your behalf. This way the reputation of your domain and the specific email inbox you're using increases.

The way this works is your email warmup provider has a network of other users that also want their email accounts to be warmed up. All the accounts are sending and responding to emails between each other, and marking the emails as 'Important'.

Before launching your outreach campaigns, you need to warm up your email accounts for three to four weeks before sending any emails. This means that if you plan to launch your campaigns soon, you need to start the warmup process well in advance.

Most Cold Email tools now include email warmup functionality. They will gradually increase the number of emails going out from your account. Starting with 5 emails per day, going all the way up to 40+ emails a day, at which point you should be good to go live with your campaigns.

After an account is warmed up, you should keep the warm-up tool on for as long as you use that account to send campaigns. This way, if the reputation of that account drops, the email warmup tool will make sure to restore it in the background for you.

Like a chef that preheats the oven before they can bake the pie, so should you ensure that your email accounts are properly warmed up and looking 'hot' before you start reaching out to prospects?

HOMEWORK: *Connect your email accounts to a warm-up tool and start warming them up. After three weeks, you'll be ready to launch your campaigns.*

Chapter 17

Personalization Formula & Positioning

W*hat does the personalization formula look like?*

The issue with Cold Email is that it doesn't unless you're completely clear on who you are, what you offer, and what your goal is. These are the six elements you can use to build a powerful personalization formula before you start writing your emails:

- Industry and Niche
- Problem, Opportunity, Or Threat
- Dream Outcome
- The Offer
- 'Why Now'
- 'Why Me'

Industry and Niche

The first element is the industry and the niche. We have already discussed how you can pick a specific industry. Using the right firmographic and demographic characteristics for every industry you're targeting.

Ideally, you're not going after an industry but a specific *niche within an industry*. You don't want to target everyone in eCommerce. You want to target fashion companies based in the US that are doing more than $1M in revenue a year!

Problem, Opportunity, Or Threat

The next step is you have to have a clear problem, opportunity, or threat laid out for them which you can help overcome. Typically this is something their industry, or their company specifically would be facing.

Here are some examples of an Ecommerce business:

- **Problem:** their current media buyer doesn't know how to run TikTok ads
- **Opportunity:** AI now allows them to offer personalized product recommendations and support.
- **Threat:** a new global competitor entered the market and is selling similar products at a discounted price, eating up their sales.

Dream Outcome

The next element is the dream outcome. The dream outcome is what happens when you're able to overcome the problem, conquer the opportunity, and manage or overcome the threat.

- *What does the specific individual I've already identified looking to achieve?*
- *What does the ideal world look like?*
- *What's the ideal outcome that they would like to get from my services or that they would like to have in their daily lives?*

If Facebook is shutting down its third-party cookies, the dream outcome for an Ecommerce business would be to have a better way to target digital audiences and track conversion from them.

Therefore, if you can clearly articulate the dream outcome and tie it to a case study of a client you've already worked with, you will have a really good recipe for success.

The key to selling to businesses is that case studies are really important.

Having a specific case study or a transformation from within a specific niche, solving a specific problem, being able to have that process done once, and then just being in the position to replicate it for other clients is where you want to be with cold email.

You don't want to run cold email campaigns trying to sell without having case studies. However, you could still do that, but you'd be aiming for different types of engagements and connections with your potential audiences, given that you don't have a transformation in place.

The Offer

What are you offering people?

The offer can make or break your Cold Email campaign. When promoting your products and services using Cold Email and performance marketing, you need to make sure your offer is optimized for those channels.

What do these optimized offers include?

They promise a specific transformation to a specific audience. They have an identified result and a clear timeline for implementation. In many cases, they have a money-back component and detail on what happens if things don't go well, just because the element of trust is not there yet.

Here are a few examples of what an offer could look like:

- *We'll fix your Meta ads attribution in 3 weeks or less or your money back.*
- *We'll help you get a 2-3x Return on Advertising Spend (ROAS) from your advertising campaign.*
- *We'll help your team work three times more efficiently using time tracking and our signature project management workflow.*
- *We will implement a 3-step process that's going to make managing your ad campaigns much easier to build, run and optimize.*

The offer is a really important component to get right. If the offer is working well, you're going to get a ton of positive replies and sales.

'Why Now'

The last two components you need with Cold Email are 'why now' and 'why me'.

Why is our company a good fit for this service?
  Why are you reaching out now?

You don't need to have both, but if you do it's the best-case scenario. People need to feel that there's a reason you're reaching out to them now. Including a sense of urgency helps tie the call to action, to an actual action that the users need to take.

'Why now' is the personalization element that helps you connect to the user you have in front of you. So *why now* could be something like:

- *With Black Friday approaching, brands are looking to optimize their ad or email campaigns*
- *Your brands are looking to send 2000 times more emails*
- *Brands are looking for a way to sell their products more efficiently*
- *With AR content being all around us, eCommerce stores are looking to implement technologies to host AR content for their best-selling products*
- *With the launch of Amazon advertising, there's a really big opportunity for businesses looking to sell through that channel*
- *With the decline of Bitcoin and the decline of the financial market, it's getting harder than ever to get access to financial investment for your business.*

So *'why now'* goes along with the problem or opportunity or threat in the industry. It's really useful because it helps make the campaign time-sensitive, and that helps you get a response.

'Why Me'

The last element is *'why me'* or *'why us'*. I call this the 'secret sauce' of cold email, and it can be the actual email personalization element. A sentence is personal to each specific prospect or company.

It could be something like:

- *I saw you're running Facebook ads, and we integrate with Shopify. Given that your business is running on Shopify, let's have a conversation on how we can help you optimize your ads*
- *It looks like you're making a big investment in Content Marketing. It would be amazing to combine that with SEO, so you can leverage the traffic from Google you've already worked hard for*
- *I saw you using Hubspot, and we recently helped a B2B client get three times more leads by implementing HubSpot forms across their website.*

These are some examples of 'why me' or 'why us', that you can include in your emails, to help you get more positive responses.

Here's a complete example of the personalization formula, put together as a cohesive email (minus the intro and outro):

- *We help eCommerce brands (**this is the niche**)*
- *Solve Facebook ads attribution (**this is the problem or opportunity**)*
- *And achieve up to 2-3x ROAS on their campaigns (**this is the dream outcome**)*
- *Through our six-step tracking mastery program (**this is the offer**)*
- *With Black Friday and Cyber Monday approaching brands are looking to optimize their campaigns (**this is the 'why now'**)*

- *I noticed you're running Facebook ads using Shopify, which we integrate natively with (**this is the 'why me'**)*

As you can see, a big part of our email is already done. Simply by defining every element of the personalization formula with specificity. If you get these elements right, crafting high-converting cold emails will become your favorite habit, and a piece of cake.

HOMEWORK: *Apply the Personalization Formula to your business and build the foundation for the perfect Cold Email.*

Chapter 18

Creating Your Cold Emails

Welcome to the heart of your Cold Email campaign: crafting the perfect copy. This chapter is your guide to transforming your offer into a compelling message that turns prospects into customers. Ready to create emails that resonate? Let's dive in!

Cold Email Mindset

There's a specific mindset that drives the strategy and structure around your first cold email that you need to keep in mind.

The most important thing I always aim for with my campaigns is to **communicate everything on the first email** I send. The first email you send is the most important one. It should contain what you can offer the other person and should initiate a conversation with them.

That's what a Cold Email is. You saying, *'Hi, this is what I do and how I can help. If it's of interest, would you like to learn more?'*

The second element is you need to include **meaningful personalization**. Traditional Email Marketers made us believe that personalization is including *'Hi {{first name}}'* in our emails. That's not it.

Make sure you address the user in a personalized way. Reference something specific they've accomplished, a post they published, an attribute of theirs, or a problem they might be facing.

This is where the personalization formula comes in handy. You want to go as custom in terms of personalization as you can. The email you send to one person should feel completely irrelevant if you sent it to someone else.

Based on the 'Mom rule', if you emailed your mom and said *'Hey mom, I loved the chocolate cake you sent me, especially the strawberry frosting'* and your dad or your siblings read the email, they would know it's not directed to them. They are not moms. *That's what we are looking to achieve.*

You also need to keep your emails short and **focused on the other person** as much as possible – no blabbering about yourself or your business.

You want to avoid starting sentences with the words 'I' or 'We'. Focus on leading with *'you'* instead. This makes everything about the email related to the prospect, not you, and increases resonance.

Something else that people always do wrong is **trying to touch on many points** and narratives within the same email. You need to focus on one topic. Ideally, the most important one. *I know it's hard but go for it.*

If you want to sell me your Facebook Ads services, don't spend a paragraph mentioning your new course, the webinar you're launching next month, or anything not relevant to the problem I'm facing: *Your ads could be performing 100x better using this strategy.*

In the same context, don't list 100 different services in one email just because you can offer them. Instead, focus on the one that solves the problem you have identified.

Being focused on your email, extends to your **call to action, or ask**. You can only ask me to take one specific next step – whether that's booking a meeting, inviting me to a webinar, asking me about my weekend, or requesting referrals from my company.

When you're asking something from your prospects, your email should be structured in a way they can answer with **one of the following kinds of responses**:

- 'Yes, I'm interested' / 'Yes, let's chat' / 'Tomorrow 4 pm works for a call' **(interested)**
- 'No, I'm not interested' **(not interested)**
- 'Hear are my thoughts on this topic' **(answering an open-ended question)**
- 'Talk to this person' **(providing a referral within their company)**

With that in mind, review your existing cold emails and restructure them accordingly.

Some of the responses you receive are still going to be things like 'unsubscribe' or 'stop', but that's not the kind of response we're aiming for.

What's the goal of a cold email?

It is to schedule a call with someone or move them forward in the sales process. You don't have enough time to close a deal with just one cold email. So you need to leverage the first email as a way to move to the next steps.

The most people are going to spend on your email is 1 - 2 minutes, and that's provided that it's super engaging and interesting. You want to establish contact with your first email, spark their curiosity, and briefly state what you can offer them – so that they ask for the next step.

In most cases, the best next step is scheduling a sales or demo call. It might be the case that you ask for a survey completion or anything else like that, but in most cases, the goal is to get a 'yes' or 'no' with regards to booking a call and getting them to know more about you and what you offer.

You can think of it as if you're going on a date with someone for the first time. If you kneel on one knee and propose to them during your first coffee date, they will most likely freak out and run. You need to act a bit more smoothly and lay the foundations to continue seeing that person.

That first – sometimes awkward – coffee date; that's the first cold email you send to someone. Now that we've discussed the proper etiquette for a first date, let's dive into the basic parts of a cold email.

A cold email actually consists of **three parts** you need to calibrate and optimize.

1. The email body
2. The email signature
3. The subject line

The Email Body

This is where most of the mistakes happen, as people get confused – and a bit overzealous – with what they should be including. Allow me to walk you through the anatomy of the cold email.

There are **five different elements:**

- **Clear Intro**: state who you are and briefly include what you're doing. Include any relevant social proof you might have earned.
- **Context and Personalization**: Why did you reach out to them and their company specifically? Why is now a good time for this initiative?
- **Dream Outcome**: What can you help them achieve? What's the big transformation you're promising them? What's your USP compared to your competitors or alternative solutions? This is also a good place to add any relevant Case Studies you have.
- **The Ask:** What do you propose to them? What's the offer?
- **Call-to-Action (CTA):** What's the next step? What do you need them to do?

This is where the personalization formula comes in handy. It's probably the only thing you need to have in mind when writing your email copy.

- Who are you reaching out to?
- What's the problem or opportunity you're helping them tackle?
- What is the dream outcome? What would they ideally want in their lives?
- What is the offer that you're sending their way?
- Why now and why that specific company?

Make a list of these questions, and then answer them on a piece of paper for every ICP you want to target. By the time you're done, most of your email copy will be ready.

Let's go through an example to see what this looks like.

Subject line: *partnership idea*

Hi, my name is Bill.

I run SalesCaptain and we scale SaaS businesses like Airtable, Clearbit, and Open AI.

Congrats on launching the Speechify iOS app! We work with Notion and I wanted to explore what a partnership looks like.

We have over 20 million users today, 85% of whom create shareable content and would be good users of your app. We have an idea for a collaboration that would benefit our and your existing customers.

If you're interested, we'll love to discuss next steps with your team.

Best, Bill

If our cold email was a cake, at this point we've built the cake – the email body. Let's now add the icing – a well-crafted email signature.

The Email Signature

The next step after you've crafted the body of an email is the **signature**. You want to keep the signature short and to the point. The signature typically includes:

- Full name
- Position at the Company
- Website and LinkedIn link

I typically only include one link in the signature. It's either a LinkedIn profile if the person reaching out has a strong social presence or a link to a landing page for the specific ICP, which includes a link to book a call.

A very simple example would be:

Bill Stathi *Founder, SalesCaptain +1 (646) 7045852*

Finally, time for the cherry on top of our cake. The subject line.

The Perfect Subject Line

We leave the subject line for last and for good reason. Once you have the email body and signature ready, the subject line should come to you quite effortlessly.

There's no need to overthink. Despite best practices from Email Marketing, you actually want to keep the subject line short, at 3-4 words maximum. The goal is to *entice* the reader to open the email.

The subject line is important because along with the sender's name it's the only thing prospects see before opening your email. So you need to make sure you make a good impression.

Here are the four main ways to write a subject line, so you don't need inspiration to write an effective one:

- Personalize based on the topic of your outreach
- Personalized based on their first name
- Personalize based on the company name
- Include a buzzword or hype word to make them curious

When personalizing based on the contents of your email, try not to give everything away. If your email is related to 'Content Marketing', you could use 'Content Marketing chat?' or simply 'Content Marketing'.

You want to avoid phrases like: 'Marketing Automation software: request for a call' or lines that would give away the purpose of your email. Here are a few examples of effective subject lines:

- Artificial intelligence
- Content Marketing chat?
- Outbound
- Question about your article on {{Magazine}}
- Meeting Request

Another way of structuring your subject lines is by including their company name. Here are some more examples:

- {{companyName}} x SalesCaptain
- Question about {{CompanyName}}?
- +1 friend request from SalesCaptain 🤍

- Quick chat about {{companyName}}?
- question for {{companyName}}

And, of course, you can always mix and match any of the above:

- Free workshop at {{companyName}}
- thought I'd reach out, {{firstName}}
- One Marketer for all, all for AI
- Reach students for {{companyName}}

One thing to *avoid* is using spam words, like 'free', '$$$', 'offer', 'cash', 'guarantee', etc, for obvious reasons – they trigger spam filters like anything else.

Regarding the use of emojis, they're fine as long as you don't overuse them. I try to avoid them in my subject lines, but make sure to A/B test if you are unsure what to do.

Different audiences require different levels of sophistication depending on their background and will respond differently to the use of emojis and more casual language in the subject line.

The last, and super important thing is to keep your subject line consistent across the entire email flow. There's a really, really good reason for this.

If you're sending a cold email and someone doesn't open it, it probably means one of the following things:

- They're not active on their email account

- They're on vacation
- It could be a public holiday where they live
- The email might have gone to their spam folder; which ideally we've avoided
- They're busy
- They didn't care
- They didn't notice it

For all these reasons, it makes sense to follow up after a few days. A Cold Email campaign doesn't finish after sending the first email. Money is in the follow-ups.

Now imagine someone sends you an email, and you don't respond. And then they send another email. And then they send a third and a fourth one. What if all those emails had different subject lines?

They will end up as different threads in your inbox. What if you didn't want to respond, didn't have time to respond, or you didn't even notice their first email?

You've ended up with four different emails from the same person. You might accidentally open email #4 in the flow, which is a breakup email, and doesn't state they reached out, or what they want from you. Figuring out what's going on can leave you very annoyed.

For this reason, it's important to keep the subject line consistent across the flow. When sending follow-up emails, they should appear as part of the same email thread in your prospect's inbox.

Whether they open the second, third, or even fourth email, they can easily trace back to your initial message, understand why you're reaching out, and decide whether or not they want to engage with you.

Aaaand there you have it! Our cake is now complete.

Terminator's Personalization Secret

Now that we've walked through the anatomy of a cold email, I can let you know one of Terminator's secrets that's going to help you rock every cold email you send out.

Terminator went back in time to protect John Connor. Specifically John. Not 'every company in the tech industry with a website.' Why am I saying that? Because what we see most of the time is people don't try to personalize.

They just will say: 'Oh, I reached out to you because you have a website.' Well, everyone has a website. That's not a specific reason you would reach out to someone. Reaching out with non-personalized copy decreases your chances of getting a positive response.

That's pretty much the secret and why it matters so much for the success of your campaign overall.

When you're writing your email copy, think like Terminator. You're sending that email because you have identified something really specific within that company that made you say, 'Oh, they could be good clients'. And based on that, you have a really good offer in place for them.

Where do you get that data? Again, look at their psychographic, techno-graphic, and demographic data and any actions they took that you can track (downloaded an ebook, attended a webinar, watched a sales video, etc.)

A second secret is to remove any guilt from yourself about sending cold emails. If you do it right and you follow the principles of this book, you will provide value to someone who needs it.

There's no reason to feel ashamed! Give your full capacity to make this happen when running your cold email campaigns.

Yes, you're going to receive negative responses. Not everyone is in a good mood. Not every negative response will be the same, but as we've discussed with the sales mindset, you have to get through those nine negative responses to get to the positive one because the one positive one can change your business or your life.

And then the last secret is you're not a spammer. You're not doing anything spammy, but also, don't act like a spammer.

Given that you're not a spammer, here are some of the **activities you should avoid** doing:

- You're not going to email people ten times when they've not responded.
- You're going to unsubscribe a prospect from your list when they said they said they don't want to hear from you again.
- You're not going to be reaching out to their team member if they have asked not to contact anyone from their team.
- You're gonna email people within reasonable work hours, and you're gonna treat them respectfully and not try to scam them.

By doing all of these things, you eliminate any reasons that could cause your Cold Email campaigns to underperform.

There's nothing wrong or illegal about Cold Email. You need to use it as a means to approach other human beings and start mutually beneficial business relationships.

If you believe that you have something of value to offer, there's nothing to worry about. You can feel good about yourself and your campaigns. You will most likely get really, really good results with Cold Email.

Chapter 19

Cold Email Templates

R eady to see what Cold Emails look like when we put everything together? Here are some battle-proven templates that we've used in our own campaigns. I'll explain why and how they work so that you can start your outreach confident that you have a solid foundation. Don't forget to add your own twist for every ICP, based on the personalization formula.

Saas Free Trial

The classic 'current solutions vs. new solution' template. The key is not to convey everything from the first email, but tease the prospects as to why a previously expensive solution is now affordable. The mention of existing solution providers strengthens the claims, and the CTA is really tempting as well.

Subject: *competitors monitoring*

Hi {{firstName}},

Here is what's wrong with Competitive Research in 2023. It costs either lots of time or money ($15k+) to do it.

Competitive Intelligence tools such as Crayon and Klue are overpriced. This leaves Product Marketers to spend countless hours searching the internet for limited insights.

Our proprietary tech allows you to track everything your competitors do for as low as $9.90 per month.

Worth a trial? Happy to set you up with a free account.

{{YourName}}

Saas Demo

Keeping it short and to the point is something I love about this email. It's literally 3 sentences long. Bonus for adding some proof in terms of the usage numbers and touching on the specific industry – agencies. Plus, the subject line matches the email body perfectly.

Subject: *icebreakers*

Hey Bill, do you use personalized 'icebreakers' in your cold emails or just the personalized images that Lemlist is so known for? :)

Asking because we're supporting 5,893 users (and counting..) including some major agencies in scaling their personalized cold outreach using AI-generated icebreakers.

Worth a peek?

Building Partnerships

Reaching out to a company in a specific industry and highlighting another client of yours from the same industry is a good move. The CTA is also what I call a 'softer CTA'. Meaning they're not trying to sell something immediately. It's easy to respond to someone who wants to send you more details.

Subject: reviews for {{CompanyName}}

Hey {{firstName}},

{{YourName}} here. {{icebreaker}}.

Launched a new reviews tool for agencies and wanted to run it by you.

Think TrustPilot, Google, TripAdvisor, Facebook reviews, etc all rolled into the one dashboard. As an agency, it allows you to offer your clients a new billable service, and for your clients, helps them get more 5-star reviews on any review site (plus much more).

Partnered with {{Agency-1}} and {{Agency-2}} recently. Would love for you to check it out, too.

Can I send through some more info?

{{YourName}}

Coaching Clients

Solid mention of past experience and expected results – the Dream Outcome is a good place to start for your first Cold Email. You need to test the CTA, of course, but the phrase *'Do you have the capacity for new clients'* has worked really well for me in certain industries before.

Subject line: *new coaching clients*

Hey {{firstName}},

Your coaching experience is impressive; thought I reach out directly :)

So I'm in the coaching space as well and using my 8-year sales expertise and our new software to bring experts like you 3-8 potential clients every day.

Do you have capacity for taking on new clients?

Best, {{SenderName}}

Hiring Sales Trigger

The quality of data you use in your outreach usually matters more compared to having the perfect copy. In this case, since we know our target company is hiring for a specific role – you can use Sales Navigator for this – it becomes really easy to tailor a message to them.

Subject: *SDR ramp-up*

I saw you're hiring for SDRs, {{FirstName}}. I imagine you're thinking about how they'll ramp.

Usually, our customers focus training on phones. But, email results lag.

We're helping reps at {{ClientName}} ramp faster. They continue improving with our in-inbox assistant.

Worth a chat? {{YourName}}

SEO Agency v1

The emphasis is on the fact that we've already done the work. There's a clear and easy-to-follow CTA, and the action itself is quite harmless. When you put in work in advance, you can share it as a loom recording on a landing page, with a button below for people to book a call.

A different variation of this email would be to have one line where they mention a specific insight from the audit, especially related to a competitor of the business.

Remember though, just because you did the work, you can't just share it as a pdf on the first email. You need to ask permission from the prospect first.

Subject line: *your Google search results*

Hey {{firstName}},

Non-branded traffic makes all the difference. Our clients average $30k+ in new monthly subscription sales from 10k a month in non-branded traffic...

We made you a custom marketing video analysis with actionable steps on how to improve your non-branded traffic for free.

If you're interested, respond with YES and I'll send it over.

Thanks, {{YourName}}

SEO Agency v2

Big emphasis on adding value and personalization here. If you do want the call you gotta put in the work. Best part is there's no CTA. You can bet though that because of the work put in, if the SEO Research is true, the prospect is going to be begging to work with you.

Subject Line: *{{First Name}} – Why {{Competitor}} is out-ranking you for {{Keyword}}*

Hi {{First Name}},

It was really interesting to search for "keyword" on Google and notice you aren't at the top of page one (you're currently #{{Current Rank}}) ...

Looks like {{YourCompetitor}} are getting all the traffic ;)

You can see proof right <u>here</u>. I've ranked a few more companies.

Not that hard to rank higher than your competitors thanks to {{positive thing about your site or SEO}}.

I've created this video to will show how. Within the first few minutes of watching you'll see it's totally doable. If there are any questions send them my way!

{{YourName}}

Cold Email Agency

Dream Outcome combined with a specific industry, along with a case study from the same industry, and a personalized icebreaker will always bring good results. Finetune your Personalization Formula and go for it.

Subject line: *hot leads for {{CompanyName}}*

Hi {{First Name}},

{{Icebreaker}}

We work with {{Industry}} companies helping them bring in sales appointments with {{IdealClients}} every single day — leaving cold calling and lunch & learns in 2020.

For instance, one of our clients generated over $500k in Sales in their first 30 days, investing only $5k directly targeting {{IdealClients}}.

I'd love to do the same for you! Mind if I send over a few times for a quick call?

Excited! Thanks, {{YourName}}

P.S. We normally bring in about 20 new {{IdealClients}} per week for our clients, but this can be scaled up or down to suit your requirements and goals.

Ecommerce Brands

Straight to the point. Short and sweet with no fluff. This is one of my first outreach emails. Touches on a specific result and includes a lot of social proof. We were able to get 12%+ Reply Rate, which is pretty big.

Subject line: *post-production time*

Hi {{firstName}},

My name is {{YourName}} and I'm with {{YourCompany}}.

We help enterprise eCommerce brands get the same product quality as Tom Ford, DKNY, and Puma while decreasing go-to-market time by 2-4x.

Would you be kind enough to point me to the person within {{companyName}} in charge of post-production?

Thanks for your help!

{{signature}}

Link Building

This is a practice that SEOs have been doing for many years now. Given how common this type of outreach is, the goal is not to start with a pitch on the first email but to build a relationship and provide value. This makes it much easier to ask for the backlink once they respond.

Subject: *Can I share your site {{firstName}}?*

Hey {{firstName}},

My name is {{YourtName}}, and I run the {{BlogName}} blog.

Real quickly I thought I'd reach out because of a piece of yours I found here: {{URL}}, and thought it was a good one.

So I thought I would ask if it will be OK that I will share it on our Facebook page and on Twitter.

{{YourName}}

Content Creators

Start with a short, effective email. Don't overwhelm them with a wall of text, and don't try to explain your entire brand story or try to flatter them with fake compliments on their 'latest post'.

Subject: *{{FirstName}} big fans of your work*

Hi {{InfluencerName}},

I'm {{YourName}} with {{BrandName}}. I came across your post on {{Topic}} and thought you would be a perfect fit for our latest campaign.

I'm giving away free {{roductName}} samples, as well as samples to give away to your followers, in exchange for 2 social media posts promoting your experience with our brand.

Are you interested in participating?

Let me know, {{YourName}}

Decision-Maker Referral

When reaching out to larger enterprises, before selling you need to locate the right decision-maker. This can oftentimes be complicated. A referral works really well in these cases. If you give the time and effort to make this a personal email, it will do the trick.

Subject line: *appropriate person*

Hello {{FirstName}}, are you the correct contact at {{Company}} to discuss {[insert topic]}? If not, would you mind letting me know who I can follow up with?

For context: {{insert valid business reason for reaching out}}.

If you are the right person for this, or you know of a more appropriate contact at {{Company}} - please let me know.

Best, {{YourName}}

Event Attendees

This is a perfect use of intent data once again. You can simply go on LinkedIn, search for relevant events, click 'Attend' and access other people going to the same event. If you have something relevant to offer, it should be fairly straightforward. In this case, the event was a Cold Email workshop.

Subject line: *outbound copywriting & {{CompanyName}}*

Hi {{FirstName}},

Noticed that you attended {{Company}}'s event on {{EventTopic}} and as someone who is likely interested in scaling outbound, I thought of reaching out.

{{YourCompany}} streamlines the entire copywriting process in order to help outbound teams launch personalized persona-driven sequences faster.

{{FirstName}}, would you be interested in learning how we can reduce your time spent on all copywriting tasks?

Best, {{YourName}}

HOMEWORK:

Select the Cold Email template that matches your use case and build your first Cold Email. I'll recommend doing this on Google Docs because it has version history and allows you to see roughly what your email is going to look like once it hits the inbox.

Chapter 20

Personalization at Scale

One of the most important elements that can help make your campaign a success, is personalizing your emails in a meaningful way.

Make each one of the emails so specific, that the recipient thinks that this email has only been created for them. So that if you send the same email to a different recipient, they won't understand how it relates to them.

You can do that by including a really specific personalization line within the first cold email in your sequence. All the other parts of your cold email remain pretty much the same.

You only need a personalization line at the start of the email. The real challenge is doing this at scale. I'm going to walk you through a system that makes it really easy.

The {{Personalization}} line should be something meaningful and real, like:

'I saw a client raving about how you've helped them for a decade. That's a longer

relationship than most couples I know.'

Or something like:

'I have just finished listening to your interview on The Hustle. Much respect for your tactics for building a 1 million dollar business. I enjoyed listening to it.'

This gets prospects hooked. They understand you've done your due diligence, you know who they are, and you're reaching out to them specifically – and blasting the same email to hundred other people at the same time.

This can have a significant impact, both on your reply rates, as well as the number of people who respond positively, and end up booking a call. It can help increase the Gold KPIs of your campaigns significantly.

How do you do that?

Most Cold Email tools allow you to include variables within your emails. These variables typically include {{FirstName}}, {{LastName}}, {{Company-Name}}, etc.

You can also create and include custom variables. I call the personalization variable I created *{{Avocado}}*. That's right, avocado. It's a fun word and it helps our team remember to always personalize – and eat their avocados.

The only questions are: *Who writes the personalized line? And where do we write it?* These are both really good questions. Let's try and answer them.

Before sending out a campaign, you need to upload the list of leads to your Cold Email tool. The prospect list includes first name, last name, company name, email address, etc.

To do personalization at scale, you just need to include one more column on your Excel sheet and name that column 'Avocado', or anything else you like. It won't make any difference.

Then, after you've built your prospect list, write one personalized line for every prospect. Let's say the first lead is Bill from SalesCaptain. The 'Avocado' column could include the following text:

'I saw you on the GrowthMentor podcast, and I loved your Cold Email strategies.'

After you're done with the line for one prospect, you can proceed with writing copy for the next lead, and the next lead, and the next lead. That's how you do personalization copywriting at scale.

You personalize every lead once, then you upload the list, and then the emails go out according to the sending schedule. Without you having to worry about anything else.

Here's what to not include in the 'Avocado' column. Avoid generic sentences like

- I'm a big fan of yours and I've been following you for years.
- I love your book. It blew me away.
- I saw you on LinkedIn and thought I reach out.
- We're in the same industry so I thought I reach out.
- I came across your profile and thought I reach out.
- My namy is Andrea and I'm with company X.

Do not use fake and shallow flattery. Instead, invest time in actually researching and writing something meaningful and unique to them.

Even if it makes launching a campaign a bit more time-consuming, you'll see that you'll have vastly different results when your personalization line is actually personal to the individual you're reaching out to.

Obviously, not all your campaigns need to include personalization. Use it for your most valuable prospects and accounts.

What's your 'Avocado' word? Share yours on Twitter, tag @billstathi and win a free Cold Email Audit and access to our templates vault.

HOMEWORK: *Download the Avocado Personalization sheet from coldemailsecrets.co/resources and write personalized lines for ten prospects.*

Chapter 21

Following Up to Get More Responses

Here's the main takeaway here: The money is in the follow-up.

Why is following up important?

Statistics have shown that 80% of sales take five follow-up emails to close. It might not be the case every time, but it doesn't hurt to be the one better prepared if you want to win the war.

Before we discuss what the follow-up flow looks like, let's have a look at why people don't respond to our emails. Despite our best efforts.

- They were busy
- They were on vacation
- It was not an important need, product or service for the company at the time
- They don't use their email account at all
- Our email got lost in their cluttered inbox
- They already have a full inbox

- They were in a bad mood
- They have focused on a different project or just bad timing

For all these reasons, it's important that we don't just exhaust our efforts in sending one cold email, but instead follow up at least 3-4 times.

How can we craft the perfect follow-up email that gets responses?

With our follow-up flow, we're not trying to convey any new information. It's just to bump the first email we sent – including the intro, why we're reaching out to them, the dream outcome, ask and call to action – right to the top of their inbox. After all, we've spent all this time and effort writing this email.

This is achieved by keeping the subject line consistent across the flow. Also, as we've already discussed, no new information or new asks should be conveyed within follow-up emails.

If your first email says: *'Let's book a demo call'*, your follow-up cannot be saying, *'Here's a webinar we're hosting today. feel free to join'*. You'll confuse your prospects badly.

If you come from the world of Email Marketing, you might also think it's a good idea to try to and 'nurture' prospects with cold emails. Please don't do that. It's a big mistake to send a bunch of content as a follow-up email to people who haven't even bothered responding to your first email.

What about sharing the link or attaching a file to a free audit or health check you did for your prospect?

If the content you want to send over is important enough, you wouldn't just share it with anyone, would you? You would first want to make it appear as important by asking for permission to send the content.

If you want to test out sending a personalized video demo, mini audit, or any other personalized resource, make the effort to present it and ask if they actually want it, before you go into the trouble of recording it for all your prospects. This can very well be the CTA of your first email.

Here's an example of how you would implement this if you were offering SEO services:

'I analyzed how your top 3 competitors rank on Google and recorded a short video which includes the five pieces of content you need to write about on your blog to outrank them. Would you like me to send it over?'

This helps in two ways:

1. The content you are about to send is perceived as more important because you are not just dropping a link to it.
2. Imagine wanting to reach out to 200 people and send them personalized videos. Instead of recording 200 videos, you can only record for those who really asked for it and thus pre-qualified themselves as higher-quality leads.

There are obviously ways to 'fake' personalized videos, though such hacks are typically short-lived and can harm your brand when people realize that the video is not actually targeted at them.

That is especially true when implemented for a huge email list, where the message ends up appearing non-personalized anyways. Better to send a link to a generic demo video, or a video based on the specific ICP you're targeting, than to send a 'fake' personalized video.

For all the reasons above, it's probably not worth it to include personalized content as a follow-up email. If it's not the focus of your campaign from your first email, it will get easily overlooked. Keep follow-up emails even shorter than the first email of your sequence, which contains the bulk of your ask and message.

This helps with readability, puts the focus on your first email, and doesn't overwhelm your prospects once they open the thread of emails you've sent them.

When it comes to setting up your follow-up emails, aim to send 3 - 4 follow-ups after the first email, and 3 - 4 days apart.

This means your prospects are going to receive 1 - 2 emails from you every work week, which is just enough to keep them aware of you, but not too much to annoy them.

A four-day delay between follow-ups has worked best for our campaigns, because it's not too pushy. You can also go with three days if you want prospects to go through the flow faster.

What happens when you set everything up and someone responds to your emails? Always make sure to pause the outreach flow when you get a response.

If you want to go the extra mile, when someone responds, you can do more than just pause the flow for that person. If the flow includes more than one prospect from the same company, make sure to pause the flow for the entire company.

This is for the simple reason that your chances of being pursued as a spammer by your target prospects increase significantly if you message their entire team, and keep following up in an automated way every week. We want our messages to appear organic, and non-automated.

The other thing you can do with your follow-up flows is included LinkedIn connection requests and visits to their LinkedIn profile for the most valuable ICPs. This way you can boost your overall conversion rates.

Why is it a good idea to connect with people on LinkedIn?

Well, it's relatively easy to optimize your LinkedIn profile in a way you're perceived as an expert in your industry. You can achieve this by engaging with other people's posts from your industry, posting thought-leadership content that shows your expertise, as well as communicating client results.

Let's dive into the **follow-up flow**, and look at some specific templates you can use.

Starting with follow-up email #1, what I call the *'Kind reminder.'*

Hey {{first name}},

Any thoughts on my previous email?

Regards, Bill

Another example would be:

Hey {{first name}},

Did you get a chance to check my last email? Bill

The goal with the follow-up email is to bump the first email into the prospect's inbox. It doesn't have to be anything complicated or include a ton of new information. It's just a simple follow-up email.

The second follow-up is where it gets a bit more interesting. I call this one the *Bonus social proof'* email.

If your company has already had a lot of success in your industry, and you have a lot of accomplishments you're proud of, you might have not been able to communicate that with the first email of your sequence. You can include it in a follow-up email.

This can be things like:

- Awards
- Certifications
- Working with really big clients (e.g. Microsoft, Samsung, Uber, etc.)
- Case studies and success stories
- Getting featured on major publications like Forbes or other industry magazines
- Speaking engagements on industry conferences
- Milestones your company has achieved

Here's an example of what this could look like for a Marketing agency:

Hi {{first name}},

I wanted to share some of the milestones we've hit so far:

- *$460,000+ in monthly ad spend managed*
- *Working with companies like ASOS, Nike, and JCPenney*
- *Clients from 10+ countries*
- *124 media buyers on board*

Let me know if this is worth discussing further!

Best, Bill

As you can see, it's to the point. It includes some bonus social proof and achievements in the form of bullets.

There's also one more email you can use as the second follow-up. I call it **'Ask for action'**, and it goes like this:

Hey {{first name}},

What would be a good time for you to discuss this on a quick 10-minute call?

How about Tuesday or Wednesday at 10:00 am Pacific?

Cheers, Bill

With this one, the goal is once again to bump the first email number to the top of their inbox. By recommending a few specific times for you to connect with the prospect, you make it easy to start a conversation.

It doesn't actually matter if you're free during those times or not. You can always get back to your prospect with the times that work for you once they've responded. The goal is to get them to respond, and this email is really effective in that regard.

There are two things to keep in mind for this one:

- You have to personalize the timezone and the days of your ask on your email to match your prospects' timezone and workdays.
- It will work best if you have clearly articulated your offer in your first

114

email.

The third follow-up is the last step of the flow if you're sending a campaign with four emails. Typically, the last step is what we call the *Break up email.*

In the past, many emailers asked their recipients to select from reasons as to why they could not respond – including humorous options like, 'My house was on fire'.

While great fun 5-6 years ago, it doesn't really work anymore – unless you're reaching out to an industry that tends to appreciate humor, or where Cold Email and Digital Marketing aren't heavily used.

The last follow-up email needs to be respectful, specific, and straight-forward. If you want to go the extra mile, you could include an additional ask on the prospect's part, in case they're not the actual decision maker.

Here's a **'Breakup email with intro request'** template:

{{First name}},

I don't want to keep hounding you if this isn't of interest.

Is there someone else on your team responsible for {{whatever you offer}}? Would you mind pointing me in their direction?

Thanks, Bill.

What this email assumes is that they're not the decision-makers, thus why they didn't respond, and also gives them the opportunity to forward your email to someone else, and say:

'Actually, Anna from the Finance team would be responsible for that. She's the best contact to follow up with. Here's her email.'

This is how we get a lot of targeted intros to our prospects' companies. And this makes it very easy for your sales teams to continue the conversation.

The other thing that this email does, is it nudges them based on their role in the business.

If I'm reaching out, let's say to the Head of Marketing, and say *'Is there someone else responsible for Marketing you'd prefer I reach out to?',* I obviously know they're in charge of marketing.

We added them to our list of prospects specifically because they work in marketing, and we assumed they are indeed the decision-makers.

By asking if there's someone else responsible, I'm getting them to reply and say, *'No, I am the one who's responsible. What can I help you with?'.* This is how you can get a positive response even on the last step of the email sequence.

You're not asking for a call or anything else, but you've just got a positive response that you can then follow up on and say: *'Given that you're in charge of marketing, here's what we do. Would you like to jump on a call?'*

Another email you can use as the final follow-up is the ***'Closing your file'*** email. It goes like this:

Hi {{firstname}},

Wanted to follow up one last time, as we're in the process of closing files for the month.

Typically, when I haven't heard back from someone it means they are either really busy or aren't interested. If you aren't interested, do I have your permission to close your file?

If you are still interested, what do you recommend as a next step?

Thanks for your help, Bill

What this email does is it lets them know that you're not gonna follow anymore. And it also gives them the option to respond with a next step that works for them, whatever that might be.

This is a really good way to end the flow and also to potentially get a positive response out of the last email.

Now what should you do after the follow-up, provided you **didn't get the response**?

Don't let the account go to waste. If you want to target Microsoft UK, for example, and the prospect you reached out to doesn't respond this doesn't mean that your chances of getting Microsoft UK as a client have failed. It's not the end of the game yet.

You can reach out to another member of the company – just make sure to wait at least two to three weeks before doing so.

This is a great time-saving tactic for your lead generation team and allows you to have an easy way to find new prospects. More importantly, you don't make the account go to waste, just because the first prospect didn't respond to one campaign.

It's worth giving it one more shot, especially if it's a big and important account.

How do you make sure you're always reaching out to the right prospect when you're targeting a big account?

The strategy you want to follow when you're building prospect lists is to start by generating a contact that's as high up in the company's hierarchy as it makes sense.

Picture this: You're a marketer offering a revolutionary LinkedIn content creation service. Your first email is to the VP of Marketing at TechTitan Inc, a thriving tech company. Two weeks go by without a response. Will you give up? Not a chance.

Move down the hierarchy from there and pick the next person that fits your ICP. Your goal is always to engage the most important decision-maker you can reach. Why? They have the authority to greenlight your proposal.

if you don't get a response the first time, you can try again. For the second attempt, shake things up. Write a new subject line, craft a slightly different offer, and assign a different salesperson for the outreach.

Always keep in mind that a lack of response isn't always a rejection. Maybe your email arrived during a hectic product launch, or while the Head of Social Media was out on annual leave.

Most people give up on a company after the first negative response, and that's one of the biggest mistakes you can make in sales. You need to be reaching out to at least up to 5 - 6 people per company per year, depending on the company size. Engaging each prospect with at least two different campaigns.

At the end of the day, if you're as determined as a hound to locate the game, you'll follow up as many times as you need to get a positive response.

HOMEWORK: *Create 3 - 4 emails to be used in your follow-up flow.*

Chapter 22

Campaign Reporting & Optimization

Now that our campaigns are up and running, we need to figure out what to track, when, and how, so that we can review the performance of the campaigns and optimize until we hit our targets.

And if you've ever done Email Marketing before, the elements you need to track won't come as a surprise. These include the Open Rate, CTR, Reply rate, Positive response rate, and Meetings booked from your campaigns.

You want to have an overview of the metrics above on a weekly and on monthly basis.

Instead of meetings booked, you can track any other conversion that makes sense to your business (event attendance, RSVP to a webinar, speaking sessions booked, etc.).

Cold Email is just like any other channel. You put in the work – sending out emails on a daily basis – and you'll get the expected result.

And you should have an overview of what that looks like, and be able to answer these questions:

- How efficient is your funnel overall?
- How many meetings are you able to book with cold email every week?
- Are you getting more positive or negative responses, and from which campaigns?
- What are the best-performing emails, campaigns, and subject lines in terms of Open Rate, CTR, and meetings booked?

Most outbound tools allow you to view the above metrics through their dashboard both for every campaign separately, and also cumulatively for all your campaigns.

If not, an integration can send data on meetings booked and positive responses to a Google sheet for you to monitor.

Writing personalized campaign copy for every ICP is something you do at least once when setting up a new campaign, but typically it's far from the last time you do it.

The first attempt is rarely the best one, or the final one. Typically, the more times you review and optimize your copy for a campaign, the better it gets.

For that reason, you have to monitor your campaigns at least once a week and optimize them accordingly.

What do you need to optimize?

We've already discussed what you need to be tracking for every campaign.

But what do the ideal metrics (open rate, CTR, etc.) look like?

For Cold Email campaigns, these metrics are the *'Gold KPIs of Cold Email'*. The standard you should be holding your campaigns against.

Here's a typical breakdown of those metrics. Keep in mind that results might differ per campaign and will depend significantly on the industry and seniority of the prospects you're targeting.

- Open rate: 60 - 70%
- CTR: 5% - 10%
- Reply rate: 7% - 10%
- Lead rate of 0.2 - 5%

This means getting between 2 to 50 leads for every thousand emails you send (lead being a positive response or meeting booked).

Having said that, the best indication of your campaign performance is the number of meetings booked and the positive replies you receive per campaign.

Why is that?

The basic reason is Open Rates can be easily manipulated. There are a lot of email providers that automatically open the emails you receive to check the content of the email and see if it's spam.

Some providers take it a step further and also click on the links within your email.

When this happens, your cold email tool might indicate that the email was opened and clicked, but actually, that was the automated spam filter checking the contents of your email.

As a result, if you're tracking open rates and click-through rates, in some industries specifically, you might see higher open rates and CTR than the actual opens and clicks by your prospects on the campaign.

On top of that, many email providers are starting to sunset pixels, the mechanism we use to track email opens.

Open rates and clickthrough rates are useful to keep in mind overall. However, they are not sufficient on their own to determine the performance of a campaign. Instead, you need to focus on the number of positive replies and meetings booked.

This is a quick and easy guide to improve the performance of your campaigns.

Reply Rate: 5% - 20% and Positive Replies: 2+

Your campaign is working well. You should be generating 2 to 50 actual leads.

Reply Rate: 5% - 20% and Positive Replies: 0

This is a really good indication that your copy is bad. People are taking the time to read the message and respond, but you haven't done a good enough job at articulating your unique selling point (USP), adding sufficient proof and curiosity, or having a proper call-to-action. You have to consider rewriting the copy of your campaign, or at least running an A/B test.

Reply Rate: 2% - 5% and Positive Replies: 0

The audience of your campaign is most likely bad. You haven't done a good enough job of connecting with them. They read your message and they ignore it.

Reply Rate: 0% - 2% and Positive Responses: 0

Both your audience and your email copy are bad. Start over by doing some audience research, define a more specific ICP, and then write your copy having a specific prospect from that ICP in mind.

Optimization Workflow

How do we optimize our campaigns? To make things simple, there are only two main elements we need to be focusing on:

- Our messaging and offer
- Our ICP (Ideal Customer Profile) and targeting

The offer you present to the market is one of the basic components that can make or break a cold email campaign.

A basic rule of thumb to help you decide on the offer is to brainstorm at least 10 different offers.

123

By now, you would understand that the more iterations of your messaging and marketing campaigns you implement, the better and more targeted the copy becomes.

It's a shame when those iterations take months to implement because you waste a lot of time when your message to the market is not optimized.

While you're copywriting your campaigns ahead of launch, brainstorm and write down at least 10 different offers.

Then pick the one or two that make the most sense and A/B test them. You need to always include an A/B test of your campaigns for every ICP.

Every ICP should include at least an A and B version of your message with different offers, a different intro, and a different call to action.

Then based on your campaign performance, you need to be updating your underperforming campaigns every two weeks.

Here's what that looks like:

If one ICP has gone through 2 rounds of updates (so three total updates on the message) and it's still not performing well, you need to update the targeting criteria for generating the leads lists or consider dropping the ICP entirely and working on a new one.

It doesn't mean that if you don't manage to get positive responses from one market you have targeted, that market is necessarily the wrong market for you.

It might be the case that the sources you use to generate prospects are not providing you with accurate data. Or that your filtering criteria is not correct. It doesn't mean you've chosen the wrong ICP.

However, if you continue trying ahead and trying to reach out to the same people, and the same kind of companies and don't get any positive responses, it's probably time to find a different way to target them or find a new ICP.

So, you pick an ICP (Ideal Customer Profile) and write specific campaign copy for that ICP.

A/B Testing Timeline

Here's the exact timeline we use that you can leverage for your campaigns:

- You test copy versions #1 and #2 by running an A/B test for 2 weeks, and it doesn't work.
- You update the copy once more, you test versions #3 and #4 of your copy for 2 more weeks, and it doesn't work.
- You test copy versions #5 and #6 for 2 weeks, and they don't work.
- You update the targeting criteria for your chosen ICP and test the new ones for 2-3 weeks.
- If none of that has worked, you can consider changing your ICP.

After one to two weeks from pushing the optimizations live each time, you should be able to see a change in the number and kind of responses you're receiving from prospects, and you should also be able to see a difference in the performance of the campaigns overall.

Meaning the reply rate, the number of positive replies, and the meetings booked have hopefully increased.

Don't worry too much if your campaigns perform sub-optimally during the first launch of your messaging and offer, or a new ICP. In fact, most campaigns that have a new element might underperform before the first round of optimization.

Additional Optimization Hacks

Marketing and messaging always get better the more iterations and the more work you put into them. One really cool hack to fine-tune your message is to leverage feedback you receive from sales calls.

This means updating your cold email copy to address objections you receive during sales calls and optimizing your copy according to people's backgrounds.

To ensure you're capturing all the necessary details, consider taking notes during your sales calls. Better yet, record the conversations and create transcripts you can review later.

Both, to make sure that every member of the sales team is using the same sales script and approach, but also to be able to recover any notes or points that you might want to include in your sales copy.

When reaching out to E-commerce stores, for example, to sell Marketing services for a client, the response we kept getting over and over again from prospects was that they had already tried outsourcing the service to an agency, and it didn't work out well for them.

So we changed the offer and messaging of our client to include a strategy session, and spending 4 hours on the campaign strategy for free, without requiring the client to sign a proposal.

That made their conversion rate skyrocket. And the client started seeing really positive results with their campaigns from that point on.

Account Health Reports

One last thing to keep in mind when it comes to reporting results and tracking the campaigns is you also have to keep track of your account health.

With Cold Email, there's always the risk of one or more accounts being marked as spam and delivered to the spam folder, especially if your campaign is not performing well because of messaging, offer, or targeting issues.

The reason for that is if people don't resonate with your message, they're more likely to report your message as spam. This means you have to keep track of your account status on a weekly basis.

If your account does get marked as spam, which is okay, pause that account from campaigns from that account for 2-3 weeks. During that period, make sure your email warmup service is still active for that account, so it can help it recover.

Then use that account again, when its deliverability has been fixed.

Most email marketing tools will include a deliverability report, which shows you out of the hundred emails that have been sent from that account, how many reached the inbox folder, versus the spam folder and the promotions tab.

So you should be good to go as long as your email account's deliverability is fixed.

That also means that for every five accounts you use for your outreach, it's good to have 1-2 warmed-up accounts as backup, so you can maintain your outreach volumes in case one of the accounts goes down.

Why Open Rates No Longer Work

Getting a 60%+ Open Rate might not matter that much anymore.

Spam filters and email clients have a habit of opening emails and clicking links, all in the name of virus and phishing checks. Particularly prevalent in enterprise software, this can lead to inconsistent open rates, especially when you're reaching out to small businesses versus larger corporations.

Then there's the issue of tracking pixels. To the uninitiated, it's a tiny, invisible image that cold email providers embed in their emails. It's their magic trick to say, "Aha! The user has opened the email!" But the trickery doesn't end there.

These pixels trigger, regardless of whether a human or a software, like a spam filter or Apple Mail, opens the email. The result? An illusion that the email is being opened, even when it's not.

So, the relevance of tracking open rates on your email campaigns is fading, fast. In fact, turning off email open tracking might just be your golden ticket to avoiding the dreaded spam folder.

'But wait,' you ask, 'How do we gauge the success of our cold email campaign without tracking the open rate?'

The answer lies in the responses and conversions you receive. Are the responses positive or negative? How many calls or demo signups did you secure at the end of the day?

Say the objective of your cold email campaign is to book calls. The best measure of its success isn't the open rate but the actual number of calls you've booked.

So, instead of looking at the open rate, which is becoming increasingly obsolete, focus on the number of conversions, and the ultimate goal of your campaigns. It's not just about opening emails, it's about making real connections.

HOMEWORK: *Download the Campaign Reporting sheet from coldemailsecrets.co/resources and fill it out with your weekly performance stats. Then, update your campaigns using the optimization workflow.*

Chapter 23

Handling Responses

O ur Cold Email campaigns have a very specific objective. To always be *getting a response*. We don't want clicks, email opens, or anything else. Just for prospects to respond.

And that response is, 'Yes, I'm interested', 'No, I'm not interested' or 'Talk to this person from our team'.

As responses vary a lot, we want to have specific messaging to handle each of those responses, both the positive, and the negative ones, the referrals, and anything else that might come up.

This way we can push for booking a call more efficiently, and maximize the number of appointments booked from our campaigns.

With that goal in mind, we need to create email templates with answers to the following questions, that our team can then use to respond to people in a uniform manner.

Request for Materials

One really common question is a request for materials. It can be in the form of the following questions:

- *Do you have any case studies you can send over?*
- *Do you have a deck with your capabilities?*
- *Do you have any reviews from existing clients?*

Put together an email with 2-3 links to the materials they requested, including some of your USPs, and then offer to walk them through the materials you sent over during a call. Here's a sample response:

Hey {{First name}},

Sure thing! Here's a quick overview of our process.

Would you have 15-20mins on Monday 24th at 10:30 am (NY) to discuss your target markets and sales strategy, and walk you through our pricing?

Best, Bill

Always try to include a next step tied to them progressing in the sales pipeline with every email. In this case, sending them the materials they requested, can be accompanied by asking for their availability to book a sales or demo call.

When recommending times to have a call, always aim to add your availability in their timezone instead of just dropping a Calendly link or a similar link to an appointment booking tool.

This shows them you've taken the extra step to research their business and cater your message to them, and people tend to respond positively to that.

Request for Pricing

The second type of response you might receive, which is an extremely common question, is requesting pricing.

This is especially true if you're selling services or things where the price definitely depends on the type of service you provide or is not necessarily straightforward, or might include a lot of ad-hoc elements.

When someone makes a request about pricing, a smart response you can give is:

Hey {{first name}},

Really good question!
   Our pricing ranges from $6-15k/month depending on the number of markets targeted, the volume of prospects engaged, and your sales infrastructure.

Would you have 15-20mins on Monday 24th at 10:30am (NY) to walk you through our pricing and discuss your target audience and sales strategy?

Best, Bill

Offering a response like that means:

- You've answered their basic question which is *'What does pricing look like?'*

- You've offered a hook for a sales call
- If there is sufficient sales intent, they will reply accordingly

Giving a specific price list or quote without demonstrated sales intent, and without a clear analysis of your prospect's current state and goals, is a really big mistake in sales.

If you haven't taken the time to understand the needs of your prospects and position your product or service correctly, they will always be uncertain as to how you can help them. Just throwing a price their way is not gonna do them any good.

Intro to Colleague

Another common response you might receive is an intro to a colleague. It typically looks like this:

Hey Bill, Talk to Richard from sales. He's in charge of bringing onboard new partners.

In that case, you can have a follow-up email called 'Intro to a Colleague', which goes something like this:

Hey Richard,

James from Marketing recommended I reach out.

We are company X, and we do Y for companies like {{Company name}}. Here's a quick overview of our process.

Would Tuesday at 6:00 PM (New York time) work for a quick call?

Best, Bill

What we do

Another question is: 'What do you actually do? How can you help companies like ours?'

For this particular case, it's good to have a two-liner of what you actually do, including some case studies. Here's an example:

Hey {{First name}},

We build and run outbound sales for B2B Service businesses.

Here are some of our case studies working with companies just like yours:

- *Case Study #1*
- *Case Study #2*

Let me know if you'd like me to walk you through everything and discuss your goals with Outbound as well as your current sales infrastructure.

Would Tuesday at 3:00 PM work?

Best, Bill

Crushing Objections

Having the answers to the above responses handy can save you a lot of time when responding to prospects, especially to those who respond positively.

For any market, though, there are always people who, are going to respond negatively. What that looks like:

'We're not looking to outsource that'
   'No thanks, we're covered in this area'
   'No thanks, we have an in house team for that'
   'No thanks, we don't have a budget'

If you spend enough time running campaigns to that particular market, you'll realize that the objections you come across can be grouped into 3-4 main categories.

What I always try to do, and what I would advise you to do as well, is to start being mindful of the objections people throw your way, whether it's on an email or during a sales call.

Make notes on the four most common objections, and then create email templates with responses to them. Next time someone responds to your call or email with an objection, you'll have something meaningful to respond to them with.

Here's the formula for handling and replying to objections successfully:

Hey Joanna,

This is completely normal. We've worked with many companies that are in the same or similar situation.

This is [how we are different] or [what we can bring to the table] or [how we can help]. Here are some companies that have adopted the change we recommend, and these are the results that they have achieved.

Would you like to continue the conversation and discuss your specific situation on a call?

Best, Bill

And here's an example from a response to a brand when trying to pitch a Paid Ads service offer.

Hi Mary,

This may make perfect sense. A lot of brands actually have in-house Marketing teams managing their advertising.

Our main differentiation is that we focus on programmatic channels and our proprietary remarketing formula, including access to additional audiences that we can plug into your existing accounts.

A lot of great companies like Asos, Zara, and Attentive have had great success working with us, and have managed to drop their CPA by 2-3x while being as profitable as before.

If this resonates, would you like to jump on a 15-minute call and discuss how we were able to help brands similar to yours?

Best, Bill

Including the questions and the answers to the top objections in your response makes it more likely that you'll end up with a positive response, after all.

This can help maximize the value of each one of the prospects you've gathered in your Prospects list, as each prospect gets more opportunities to convert.

In most cases, you can get a campaign manager to respond to these emails and schedule the calls on your calendar, especially given that this is mostly repetitive work, which can be easily delegated once you build the right message templates.

Initially, it might be a bit of back and forth between yourself and your SDRs to fine-tune these messages. But after 2-3 weeks, in most cases, you should be able to respond to 90% of the emails you receive and be able to book more meetings.

The ultimate goal of an Outbound sales campaign is not the sending of emails, or even the automation of the sending part. Once you have built the basic flow of your email campaign, you need to automate the tedious, repetitive tasks, so you can focus on selling and closing deals.

HOMEWORK: *Create a Google Doc and build your canned responses based on the emails you receive.*

Chapter 24

Cold Email Automations

One positive element of selling through digital channels is that you can automate many tedious tasks that would otherwise require a lot of human effort – freeing up time so you can scale campaigns faster.

Here are five foundational Cold Email Automation flows that you can implement to maximize the efficiency of your campaigns while ensuring you don't annoy the people you're targeting.

1. Unsubscribe lead on reply
2. Add deal to CRM on positive reply
3. Send a notification to the Sales team on reply
4. Update report on positive leads
5. Follow up on calls booked

The tools you're going to need for all these automations are Zapier and any Cold Email tool and CRM that integrates with it. Visit coldemailse-crets.co/resources to download the pdf with automations, including links to copy all of them directly to your Zapier account.

Let's go through the automations one by one, starting with 'Unsubscribe on reply'.

Unsubscribe Lead on Reply

When someone from a specific company replies to your email, whether it's a positive response or a negative one, you want to immediately stop the campaigns for all prospects from the same company.

Let's assume you receive a positive response, like 'Let's have a call next Monday at 2:00 PM'. It would be counterintuitive to continue messaging people from that company, or even the same individual, given that they've already responded.

So, when someone responds, the first thing to do is pause the campaign for that person and then ideally unsubscribe their company from your campaigns.

In case you get a negative response, or someone requests to be unsubscribed, you should definitely do it. You don't want to annoy other people from their company.

Add Deal to CRM on Positive Reply

When someone responds to an email, use their contact details and the content of their response to create a deal or task in your CRM, for someone to review and respond to that message.

Why is that important?

The goal is for the sales team to be able to respond to the positive messages received in a timely manner – ideally a few hours after the initial response – while archiving negative responses.

In most cases, your prospects might not end up booking a call with your sales team right away – that's why you need a system that gives you access to the list of interested prospects, so you can follow up with them until they've booked a call.

Many CRMs actually include both the ability to keep track of your sales pipeline, as well as Email Marketing features that can send mass emails. Ideally, you want to use a separate CRM and Cold Email sending tool.

Thanks to Sales automation technologies, you can be using any CRM you want, and still, run your cold outreach campaigns from a different tool. As long as you have a process for managing positive replies, and moving the leads in the CRM after they respond, you should be fine.

To manage campaign replies, you want someone from your sales team to go through the responses in the CRM at least once a day - either at the beginning or the end of the day - and follow up with each lead accordingly.

If you're not able to separate positive and negative replies and have to add both in your CRM as deals, you can use a separate pipeline stage, which we typically call 'Incoming Leads'. Your sales team can go through it once a day, and archive deals from leads that responded negatively.

Send a Notification to the Sales Team on Reply

When someone responds to your campaign, either positively or negatively, this automation allows you to send a real-time notification, through a channel like Slack, Microsoft Teams, or even WhatsApp.

When running campaigns it's important to have a feel of how many responses you receive on any given day, what time of the day this happens, as well as having the ability to glance quickly at some of the responses.

If one day you receive fewer responses, or more responses than usual, your 'notifications channel' will give you a hint about it. That's why we typically call this 'campaign heartbeat'.

This also allows you to monitor things like your campaigns getting paused, one of your email emails getting blocked, or launching a new campaign and getting a lot of negative responses at once.

For the same reason, sending notifications to the team for calls booked is really important, given that the ultimate goal of your campaigns is booking calls with people you reach out to.

Receiving notifications about calls booked is an easy way to be in the know regarding your overall campaign performance.

Update Report on Positive Replies

You need to be able to go through all the responses you received and categorize them into positive responses, negative responses, and calls booked. Having them all in one Google Sheet makes it so much easier, and can be automated entirely.

For every campaign that you're running and for Cold Email as a channel, you need to be keeping track of your conversions on a weekly basis. Here's an example:

- Emails sent: 100
- Total responses: 14
- Positive responses: 8
- Negative responses: 6
- Calls booked: 5

Automating the gathering of reporting data allows you to review the performance of your campaigns at a glance and perform any necessary optimizations. It is an important flow to have in your arsenal.

Follow Up on Calls Booked

When prospects book a call on your website or through the calendar link in your emails, you want to make sure you're not don't continue reaching out to them. You also want to follow-up with them and ask 2 - 3 engagement questions.

These questions are not for further qualification of the prospects. Qualification happens once when building your prospect lists. Instead, they are for uncovering hidden information about your prospects and their company. Information that's not available online, that you can use during your sales call.

Here are some question examples you could use:

- Are you doing any Outbound/SEO/Email Marketing right now?
- What CRM are you using?
- What is your average ad spend per month?
- Do you have a dedicated project management expert in-house?
- Have you run Cold Email campaigns before?

The answers to those questions allow you to be more prepared for the call, have more specific insights to share with them, and a more personalized pitch that's going to keep them engaged and increase your conversion rate.

The questions and the back and forth-keep prospects engaged with you till the day of the call. The reason to keep prospects engaged is that people don't buy with just one touch point, especially for higher ticket sales. It typically takes 5-6 touches to establish trust and build the foundations for a sale to happen.

A really good starting point for building that relationship, besides producing and sharing content, is following up when someone books a call. As soon as a prospect responds to your questions, you should respond back to them.

Bonus points if your response comes in the form of a video recording embedded inside an email, and not a plain old email.

And there you have it! These are the most important, and time-consuming tasks your team doesn't have to worry about anymore. As AI advances, a lot more activities will be easily automated, allowing BDRs to focus even more on personalization.

HOMEWORK: *Visit coldemailsecrets.co/resources to download the Cold Email Automations pdf, including links to copy all of them directly to your Zapier account. Then, sign up for a free Zapier account and set up your Cold Email automations.*

Chapter 25

The Cold Email Expert's Toolkit

T here are a number of tools that can make your life easier when you're doing Cold Email or Outbound Sales in general. Here is what we're going to go through:

1. Data Sources
2. Data Scraping Tools
3. Data Enrichment Tools
4. Personalized Intro Line Copywriting
5. Email Sending tools
6. Marketing Automation tools
7. CRMs
8. Appointment Scheduling Tools

You can find the list of my favorite Cold Email tools at coldemailsecrets.co/-tools

Data Sources

If you're looking to build prospect lists for your campaigns, you need at least one database to go through and select the right prospects, using the criteria you have established when building the Ideal Customer Profile.

The typical workflow includes the following steps:

1. Select 2-3 relevant data sources
2. Identify the right companies using firmographic and technographic data
3. Then dig a bit deeper to find the specific individuals from those companies that match your Ideal Customer Profile criteria

There are different databases and different data processing flows you can put together to find and build really targeted prospect lists. Here are a few ideas on the kind of targeting you can do, and the types of data sources that exist:

- **Local leads data:** Includes companies that operate in a specific region (e.g. dentists, plumbers, psychologists, car dealerships, etc.). These data sources typically scrape their data from Google Maps.
- **Tech stack data:** Includes companies that use a specific web technology, like a CRM, an Email Marketing tool, a Website builder, and more (e.g. Hubspot, Google Analytics 4, Facebook Pixel, Shopify, etc.). You pick a technology and can see a list of all the websites using it.
- **Funding data:** Includes companies that have raised funds, including seed funding, startup details, investor data, and even companies looking to get funding.
- **Intent data:** Includes companies looking for a specific topic, service,

or technology (e.g. a company looking for a CRM, Web Development services, etc.)

- **Ecommerce platform data:** Includes a list of websites and companies using a specific Ecommerce platform (e.g. Magento, Shopify, WooCommerce, etc.). This is a subset of tech stack data, specifically for companies looking to target Ecommerce businesses.

The actual magic happens when you can combine and cross-reference data from multiple data sources e.g. target Ecommerce stores (that use Shopify, aka technographic data) that have raised more than $2m in the last year (funding data).

By leveraging more complex workflows like this, you create targeted audiences and prospect lists that boost your Cold Email CTR and reply rates.

Data Scraping Tools

After you have identified a list of companies that makes sense for you to target, it's not always necessary to collect their profile and contact details one by one.

Let's say, for example, that there's a SaaS conference taking place in a few months, and on the conference's website there is a list of companies and individuals attending the event. If you are targeting SaaS companies, having this list of companies would be a goldmine.

Or there could be a list of sellers on a specific online marketplace, and you're looking to target those sellers and offer them your Marketing services.

You can use data scraping tools to get the list of those companies much faster. It works by defining the list of companies you want to download from a particular website or database inside the scraping tool, then automatically collecting and exporting the data as a CSV or Excel file.

After you have the company list or the attendees' list, you can use LinkedIn or a similar platform to get a list of contacts from those companies and add them to your campaigns.

Data Enrichment Tools

Assuming by now that you have put together a list of prospects you want to reach out to, you'll need to find their contact details. This is where these tools come in handy.

Data enrichment tools allow you to populate contact details, including the prospect's full name, email address, phone number, company name, LinkedIn URL, and additional personal contact details.

Using these tools, you can start from a list that only includes: people's first names, last names, and companies and then end up with a complete prospect list that you can use to target your ideal clients through email, LinkedIn, text messaging, and other channels.

Data cleansing and email verification tools allow you to verify that the contact details you gathered in the previous step are correct. It's important that every email address is still used by the individual it belongs to and that an email can actually be delivered to that address.

This helps keep your deliverability rate high and your bounce rate low when running your cold email campaigns. Ideally, you would want to have a deliverability rate of 98% or above and a bounce rate of 2% or lower.

You can also use data cleansing and enrichment tools to verify the contact details of existing prospect lists you might have, especially if your campaigns are experiencing high bounce rates.

A high bounce rate means that a lot of email addresses from your list are not correct. This can be caused mainly by two reasons. Either because you never verified that the email addresses you collected are correct or because you're using an old list of prospects, which typically includes people who switched companies, their inboxes are no longer active.

Personalized Intro Line Copywriting

When you're reaching out to someone, you need to build a relationship with them before selling. A good way to achieve that is by *personalizing* the beginning of your email based on who they are and what their background is.

This can include elements from their personal LinkedIn profile, like their latest posts, any career moves, their profile description, their Twitter status, or any significant company updates.

You can do this manually, one by one for each of the prospects you want to reach out to. You would visit their social media profiles, and enrich each email individually.

You can also use AI tools to automate a big part of that process and create personalized intro lines automatically, in bulk for an entire list of contacts.

Here are some **examples** of personalized intro lines, along with some custom subject lines for every prospect:

- **Subject:** *Your CSNewswire publication*
- **Email:** *Hey John, Bill here. I read on CSNewswire that you're expanding visibility into the third-party ecosystem. I think it's a great idea to get a deeper understanding of the risks that are out there.*

- **Subject:** *AdOps feedback*
- **Email:** *Hi Amanda, I loved your LinkedIn post on the risks of outsourcing Ad Operations – it was really insightful. I'm glad Databox took the time to build an entire playbook for successfully outsourcing your ad ops team.*

- **Subject:** *multi-channel prospecting*
- **Email:** *Hi Bill, I noticed your expertise in multi-channel prospecting. What has been your biggest challenge in getting your team to adopt a multi-channel approach?*

- **Subject:** *Thoughts on your first 90 days*
- **Email:** *Hi Niklas, Congrats on finishing your first 90 days as a Junior Account Executive. What are the top things you've learned in your first 90 days as a JA?*

- **Subject:** *daily LinkedIn posts*
- **Email:** *Email: Hi Kevin, You've been posting on LinkedIn every day for the*

past 2 months. What has been the impact of your daily posts on your growth this year?

- **Subject:** *Outbound marketing tools*
- **Email:** *Hi Anna, Noticed that you have great experience in outbound marketing. What are the top three tools in your Sales stack?*

As you can see, the intro lines can be quite interesting and catchy, but just because you're using AI it doesn't mean you're off the hook and you can automate the entire thing.

You still need someone to do a quick review of every intro line and make sure it's coherent and meaningful. That person can be your BDR or your team of BDRs who manage and run the outbound campaigns.

At this point, I need to note that just because you added personalized intro lines, it doesn't mean that you have built a relationship with the other person.

This is just the first step, in a series of many steps you need to take in order to establish a meaningful relationship that can lead to a sale.

It's even more so if you're trying to sell to enterprises and large businesses, where deals move much slower, and sales take a longer time to close anyway.

Email Sending Tools

It goes without saying that you need specialized tools to send your outbound campaigns. You shouldn't be using MailChimp, Hubspot, or similar Email

Marketing tools to do the sending.

Not only because it's against their terms of service but also because they are not optimized to always reach the inbox and perform well, especially with 'cold' contacts.

Cold Email tools also include additional features like link tracking, click tracking, and having specific email-sending windows within the day, as well as sending from a personal email address.

As you might have figured out by now, cold email doesn't come from a generic marketing@company.com account but the email address of an individual. Cold Email tools connect to actual Google, Microsoft, and Zoho inboxes, and send out emails in a way that it doesn't appear as a mass message campaign.

They also warm up each of the inboxed for the emails you use, making sure that your emails will always end up in the inbox folder. And this is a really important functionality to have, making it a non-negotiable to pick a Cold Email tool instead of a more generic email marketing tool.

You can check out coldemailsecrets.co/resources for the up-to-date list of my favorite Cold Email tools.

Marketing Automation Tools

These tools are complimentary, but they're pretty useful for running and optimizing campaigns at scale.

We've already seen how a lot of the activities that require manual effort, like unsubscribing people who responded to your campaigns or booked a call from your Cold Email tool, classifying email replies, as well as reporting for the campaigns themselves, can be automated and save you a lot of time.

You can check back on the chapter on Cold Email Automations for a full list of the activities, as well as a breakdown of the flows you can implement using Marketing Automation tools.

CRMs

Another category that's especially interesting when it comes to tracking the results of your outbound campaigns, and the performance of your sales team, as well as having clear sales attribution, is having a CRM.

Most B2B companies track their Marketing and Sales activities through a CRM and eventually turn leads into deals that move through a Sales pipeline.

In terms of an outreach campaign, your CRM is the place to drop the prospects that respond positively or book calls with your sales team. Here, you can follow their journey throughout your sales pipeline, monitor conversations, and push for the sale.

Appointment Scheduling Tools

One of the primary goals of an outbound campaign can be to book a sales or demo call with someone from your team. Having Appointment scheduling tools allows you to make things far easier by automating the manual part of the process.

From Cold Email tools to data enrichment and call scheduling, using these tools is optional.

However, they can save you time, make your life easier, and allow you to scale your campaigns faster without having to hire more employees to run everything manually.

You can find a full list of my favorite tools at coldemailsecrets.co/resources.

Chapter 26

Is Cold Email Legal?

The most common question I get from people regarding Cold Email is: *'Is this even legal nowadays?'*. For the most sophisticated ones, the question might be whether the GDPR, the CCPA, or similar regulations restrict Cold Email as a business activity.

The short answer is that Cold Email is still perfectly legal. Having said that, you should always consult your legal team when it comes to compliance with privacy laws and regulations, as these tend to differ based on your region and the markets you're targeting.

When it comes to privacy and data protection laws, the GDPR is one of the most strict regulations that exist. Still, it doesn't restrict sending Cold Emails. As long as they meet certain requirements

These requirements are related to the processing and storing of personal data, as well as to data security in general. They were put in place primarily to ensure personal data are kept safe, that people can handle how their data are being used, and that appropriate consent is given when that data is being used.

Legitimate Business Interest

The most important thing you have to do to comply with the GDPR when doing Cold Email, is being able to prove that there's a **legitimate business interest** in contacting the person you are reaching out to.

Here are some reasons that provide legitimate business intent for your business to reach out to another business:

- Your product or service can help support the business goals of the prospects.
- You offer a service that can help the target company increase its revenues, make their lives easier, or optimize its processes.
- The prospect has invested recently in advertising and your product service can help them optimize their Media Buying.
- The prospect's company is hiring a Sales Manager and you reach out to the HR Manager of that company to offer a software product that can speed up their recruitment process.
- The company is hiring a Sales Executive, and you reach out to the HR Manager of that company to offer them a product that can speed up their recruitment process.
- A Head of Marketing just got hired at a DTC brand with a large ad spend that's not active on TikTok yet, and you reach out with regards to your TikTok Ads services.
- Someone from your prospect's company visited your company listing on Clutch, Capterra, and G2, or browsed through the Case Study pages on your website. Based on that insight, you assumed they were interested in your services and decided to reach out to the relevant decision-maker from that company and present your products and services.
- Your prospect is looking to expand their capabilities in an area that is relevant to your product or service (e.g., a retail store looking to

introduce contactless self-checkout).
- You got to know about a specific prospect and their company's needs from your network.
- You have previous clients from the same industry, and you're confident you can deliver similar results to companies from that industry.

Let's assume you've been working with companies from the construction industry. If you also reach out to someone else from the construction industry because you believe you're able to help them based on your background and experience, you should be covered with regard to the GDPR.

Going after businesses from industries you have experience with is also a really good way for your business to grow.

Another case could be that you got to know about a prospect from your network. A business partner introduced you to someone and said *'Jo is the person you should speak to from SalesCaptain because they're looking for a Marketing agency, and maybe you can help them.'*

Easy and Quick Way to Unsubscribe

The second element of GDPR to adhere to is **providing an easy and quick way for prospects to unsubscribe** or opt out of your campaigns.

Adding an unsubscribe link at the bottom of your email should ensure compliance. Most Cold Email tools will allow you to add the unsubscribe link automatically, and this is the most direct and quick way for prospects to opt-out.

Another way for prospects to unsubscribe is by including at the bottom of your email a phrase like: *'Our campaigns are free to reply. If you're not interested, then reply 'not interested'. We will remove you from our mailing list and database right away.'*

Including an unsubscribe link might be a trigger for some email providers to classify your email as spam or promotional. However, other email providers like Microsoft 365, might classify your Cold Email as spam if it doesn't include an unsubscribe link, so be mindful of the approach you choose.

When it comes to follow-up emails, as long as your follow-ups don't violate any of the GDPR rules and adhere to the same principles as the first email, it's perfectly legal to send them.

Now, you might be thinking: *'What if my business is based in the US? Does the GDPR actually affect me?'*

Given that the GDPR is designed to protect EU citizens, it's not really a matter of where your company is located. It's about *whose* personal data you process.

If your company is based in the US but some of your clients, partners, subscribers, or prospects are EU citizens, or you're targeting EU countries, you should process their data in a way that is compliant with the GDPR.

Now, regarding the CAN-SPAM Act and similar regulations in different countries, if you treat your Cold Email activities with the same standards that the GDPR requires, you should be covered in 95% of the cases.

It's critical that you adhere to the privacy standards and regulations of each country you're targeting in your outreach, or that your company is based in, so make sure that you seek proper legal advice when it comes to compliance.

One last dilemma is whether Cold Email is an ethical business practice. Even if it's legal. To this day, a lot of people correlate Cold Email to spam, and in some ways they're right.

Cold Email is nothing more than the act of connecting with people and companies for the purpose of providing value. Same as you might start a conversation with someone you meet at a conference or on the street.

If you're respectful with Cold Email, have a legitimate interest in helping others, and the goal of ever establishing high-value relationships, you should be alright.

Whether you use it to sell a service, help people achieve a specific goal in their professional lives, or educate them about something they've expressed interest in. There's no reason why you shouldn't leverage Cold Email in your business. It's one of the foundational tools of human communication in the online world. And you should definitely be utilizing it.

Chapter 27

Campaign Planning

W hen running Cold Email campaigns for a while, you will eventually start reaching out to more than 1,000 prospects per month.

Once you do, campaigns become more complex and harder to manage. At that point, you also need to use multiple email accounts to reach out to all prospects. Campaign planning can add structure and discipline to your outreach.

A Campaign Plan is a worksheet that contains the following elements:

- Campaigns you're going to run on a given month
- Which ICPs you're targeting with every campaign
- How many leads are going to be assigned to every campaign
- Which email accounts are assigned to every campaign

You can download the Campaign Planning worksheet at coldemailsecrets.co/resources.

By reviewing your Campaign Plan at the beginning and toward the end of each month, you're able to plan the campaigns better for the next month. You can also combine it with campaign performance data to optimize results based on the current month's outcomes.

Having a Campaign Plan also allows you to create and set quarterly sales goals, and also address any additional sales opportunities that might appear. For example, reaching out to people who attend a specific event on a given month, like Web Summit.

Your Campaign Plan can also act as a record of all the experiments and campaigns you run, so you can compare them and be able to optimize in the long run.

The way I typically advise engaging in Campaign Planning is doing it once a month, at the beginning of the month or towards the end of the previous month, for the month that follows.

During the planning session, you create the plan using the data from the previous month, set your performance goals, and then you're good to start implementing the plan.

Here's the Campaign Planning process breakdown:

1. Define the ICPs
2. Define Campaigns
3. Define the number of leads per campaign
4. Assign an email account to every campaign
5. For every 800-1000 prospects, use a different email account
6. Plan the next steps to get the campaigns live

Let's break down each part of the process, and get your Campaign Plan ready.

Step #1: Define the ICPs

We start by defining the target audiences or the ideal customer profiles, as well as the specific targeting criteria for each of the segments you want to reach out to during the coming month.

Step #2: Define Campaigns

Then, we define the campaigns we're going to run. Every campaign is mapped against one specific ICP or target audience. By looking at past campaign performance, you can decide how to best allocate your leads and sales efforts for the coming month, and whether you need to brainstorm any new campaign or angle ideas.

Step #3: Define the number of leads per campaign

The next step is to allocate the number of leads for every campaign. The important questions to answer here are:

- Which campaign do I want to put more leads on or fewer leads on, based on the source I'm using?
- How many prospects can my team generate in total every month?

Step #4: Assign an email account to every campaign

Based on the number of leads on each campaign, you need to assign an email account to every campaign. As a general rule of thumb, for every thousand leads you add to a campaign per month, you'll need to use a different email account.

Given the sending limits for each individual email account, and in order to keep your account safe, you should only be reaching out to 800 - 1,000 prospects from every different account every month.

Step #5: For every 800 - 1,000 prospects, use a different email account

After you've done that, you need to create a forwarding address to use on all the accounts. This ensures that whenever each of these accounts receives an incoming email or reply, that message is forwarded to your team's sales emails or even CRM, so they can respond in real time.

Step #6: Plan the next steps to get the campaigns live

The last step includes making a plan for generating the leads. That includes list building, updating the campaign copy, creating copies for any new campaigns you have defined, and also setting up the campaigns.

The Campaign Plan is essentially your single point of reference, helping you plan your Outbound campaigns for every month. You can also leverage it to structure your team and workflows around that plan, adding goals to build and manage the assets you need to run campaigns successfully.

That's it!

You now have a roadmap and a specific process that allows you to set campaign goals, build a plan for achieving those goals, and track the results along every step of your campaigns.

Having a Campaign Plan is a vital part of running Outbound campaigns. It's necessary, although no one really talks about it. You don't want to be running around without a plan because, without a campaign plan, it's like trying to find the exit in a room that's pitch black.

HOMEWORK: *Download the Campaign Plan worksheet from coldemailsecrets.co/resources* and build your Campaign Plan for the next month.

Chapter 28

Cold Email on Steroids

C old Email is not just about setting up campaigns and sending emails to prospects. There are additional strategies you can implement to maximize the results of your campaigns.

It's the same thing as trying to build a bridge and then adding lights on top of the bridge to make sure people can see where they're going. These are the strategies I call 'Cold Email boosters.' It's things like

1. Optimized Thank You Page
2. Warm Calling
3. Personalized Inbound Follow-up
4. Segmented Follow-up Flow
5. Sales Call Video Follow-up
6. Using a CRM for Funnel Tracking
7. Paid Ads warmup
8. Content for Authority Boost

These activities can boost your sales process – just make sure that the maximum number of people you reach out to end up booking a call and push leads through the sales pipeline more effortlessly.

Optimized Thank You Page

The first one is having an optimized **Thank You page**. There are so many arguments and objections you can cover during a 30-minute call. The way to solve this, and increase your close rate, is by starting the education as soon as when a prospect books a call.

When they book that call, send them to a landing page that includes the following type of content:

- The value proposition of your business by specific industry
- An in-depth walkthrough of your system and the mechanism (processes, tools, etc.) to help your prospects achieve the result you promised them
- Showcase results and testimonials from existing and past clients
- Provide authority content, for instance, your business being interviewed by a major publication or receiving industry awards
- Cover the three most common objectives that people mention on sales calls in a FAQ-style section

Your goal is to have people show up on the sales call or demo call already warmed up, having gone through most of the information they need to understand how you can help them.

This allows you to spend your time on the call focused on the sales process. Diving deeper into the prospect's use case, responding to any questions, guiding them toward the best solution for their business, guiding them on price, and eventually closing the sale.

The right thank you page essentially increases your close rate during the call. Especially if it includes a video of someone from your sales team walking the potential client through the solution.

The more times people engage and interact with you, the more value and authenticity you bring to the table, the stronger your connection with them is going to be, and the easier to close deals.

Warm Calling

The second strategy is doing **Warm Calling**. A lot of people ask whether it makes sense to combine Cold Email with Cold Calling, the process of making a list of prospects and then picking up the phone and calling them to try and secure meetings.

I'm not saying this approach doesn't work, especially if it's part of an orchestrated campaign, but if you want to call people on the phone, the most valuable activity you can do is warm calling, and not cold calling.

Warm calling is calling people who have already booked the call. You want to call them within the hour of booking the call, to confirm the appointment and ask them 2-3 additional questions.

The goal here is exactly the same as with the Thank You page, to start building a relationship with them, make them feel that there's a human touch in the process, and make them familiar with the process of engaging with your company.

As a bonus, you also gain additional data points to be used during your sales call. The call script can go like this:

- **BDR:** *Hi, this is {{name}} from {{company}}, following up to confirm your call with {{name}} for {{date & time}}. Does the time still work for you? It shouldn't be more than 30 minutes.*
- **Prospect:** *Yes, all good.*
- **BDR:** *Amazing! To help make the most out of our call, would you mind if I ask you 2 short questions?*
- **Prospect:** *Go ahead.*
- **BDR:** *Thank you, {{firstName}}. Are you currently running any Facebook ads?*
- **Prospect:** *Yes, it's one of our main marketing channels.*
- **BDR:** *Good to hear! And what is your average monthly ad budget? Between $1-5k, $5-10k or more than $10k?*
- **Prospect:** *Usually it's around $5-6k.*
- **BDR:** *Amazing, {{firstName}}. I'm going to pass everything to {{name}} so he can personalize your call accordingly. Any questions you might have in the meantime, don't hesitate to reach out. Have a great rest of your day!*

Personalized Inbound Follow-up

When someone books a call, in addition to warm calling them, it's always a good idea to send them a personalized email. This is something one of your sales reps can take over.

Acknowledge them for booking the call and use the information they provided on the booking form – plus your knowledge about their company and their social media updates – to provide value before the call.

You can also send them the call agenda, answer any initial questions they might have, or address any objections – so you can keep the call focused on PERSONAL ELEMENT REGARDING TOPIC.

This step helps increase the chances of your prospect showing up to the call with a more positive attitude toward you and your company.

Segmented Follow-up Flow

Sometimes, when a prospect books a call, it's scheduled for one or two weeks later. You don't want them to go cold during that period and forget why they even booked a call with you.

Before implementing a follow-up email flow, I had prospects show up on the discovery call and tell me things like, *'I don't really remember why I scheduled the call, but okay, tell me what your business does.'*

You don't want that.

After sending them the personalized email, you want to continue following up with additional messages. Sending content to build trust, establish your authority in the industry, and educate prospects.

I call this the segmented follow-up because the content for the sequence using one or more of these points needs to be personalized:

- Their #1 goal
- A problem they're facing
- An opportunity in the market
- The type of business they run

For example if you serve both B2B SaaS businesses and E-commerce brands, then create separate versions of your follow-up flow that touch on USPs for each niche.

Here's what it can look like:

'We collaborate with Ecommerce brands who make between $100k - $500k per year in sales, and this is how our Advertising Accelerator program can help.'

Or, *'We've worked with high-growth B2B SaaS startups coming out of YC, and this is how we can help.'*

You should start sending this flow right after the initial follow-up email. Ideally, you want the flow to run till the day of the meeting. This means that the follow-up flow should be at least two weeks long, with emails spaced three to four days apart.

Here's what the flow can look like:

- Day 0: Call booked - No Email
- Day 1: Personalized Follow-up
- Day 2: Follow-up #1 - Our Secret Recipe to Success
- Day 5: Follow-up #2 - Case Study #1
- Day 8: Follow-up #3 - Crushing Objection #1
- Day 11: Follow-up #4 - Crushing Objection #2
- Day 14: Follow-up #5 - Case Study #2
- Day 17: Follow-up #6 - Work Samples
- Day 20: Follow-up #7 - Crushing Objection #3

With such a flow in place, you position yourself as someone who cares about your prospects and is a credible resource for the specific industry topic. As a result, your prospects become far more likely to attend your sales call with a positive attitude toward your business.

If you don't have a follow-up flow in place, there is no need to go nuclear. You can start with one main, non-segmented flow for all prospects, then create additional, segmented flows as your sales process evolves and you validate your positioning and niches targeted.

Sales Call Video Follow-up

The question is: *When is it a good idea to send a personalized video message?*

And the answer is: if you're going to dedicate time to do that, the most valuable step in the sales process is when your prospect is in the hottest state, and that's right after the sales call.

This includes following up with a one to two-minute video sum-up of the call and the next steps. Once again, this can help increase the feeling of proximity they have to you and your business, and make them more receptive to your message.

You can use Vidyard or Loom to easily record these videos from your desktop, and even walk the prospect through a specific document or flowchart during the recording if necessary.

Using a CRM for Funnel Tracking

Using a CRM to track the Outbound Sales funnel, from the moment someone responds to your emails or books a call, until you close a deal, is a must in order to have good attribution of your closed sales.

This allows you to optimize the efficiency of your sales team and your post-response flow. Here are the CRM stages you can use:

1. Positive response
2. Call booked
3. Proposal sent
4. Follow-up call booked
5. Final discussion (optional)
6. Closed won
7. Closed lost

You'll need to optimize these according to your business' needs and current sales workflows, but it's a good flow to get you started.

Prospects that book calls with you, should skip the 'Positive response' stage and go straight to 'Call booked'. The percentage of people who end up booking a discovery call after receiving your emails depends on five factors:

- Clarity of your business positioning
- Your ability to convey information clearly via email message
- Your team's timely responses and follow-ups to those who respond
- Website quality
- LinkedIn profile quality (and company page if this is linked in your email)

Often, we overlook the last two points. It's true that Cold Email doesn't always require a good website to work as a channel. However, if you're mostly targeting enterprise companies, a solid LinkedIn profile and web presence can play huge roles in your campaign success.

A good test of your online presence is to compare the quality of design and language of your site with those of your ideal clients and competitors.

Getting back to the main point, the conversion rate from 'Email sent' to 'Discovery call booked' is a powerful metric and definitely worth tracking and optimizing against.

Using a CRM is the most efficient way to make this happen. Therefore, don't sleep on your positive responses! Make sure you're tracking them and that you have a solid sales process in place. Also, know the exact percentage of people that go from positive responses to booking a call every single week that your campaigns are running.

Paid Ads Warmup

A big boost to campaign performance is doing paid ads warmup – what I call *Double Targeting*.

This includes running remarketing ads using the email lists you've put together, or doing Account-Based Marketing (ABM), running paid ads that target specific companies and specific departments within those companies.

In a sense, what you're doing here is reaching out to and targeting companies via two different channels: email and social media (most likely LinkedIn and Facebook).

This helps maximize the amount of times prospects see your message and brand in a specific amount of time. You become top of their mind and increase the chances that they open your emails.

In a nutshell, you get more real estate in their lives, and this can lead to better response rates and increased perception of your company as a solution provider at the same time.

Content for Authority Boost

The last booster is leveraging content to boost your authority as an expert and generate demand from the market.

Running Cold Email doesn't mean you shouldn't also be doing any other marketing or sales activities. Cold Email can capture the market demand your business has generated but generating that demand needs content..

You might have the best solution and most efficient business in the industry – however, it's not going to help unless you showcase it to your potential clients.

One activity you should be doing is putting together your best ideas, processes, and templates and producing at least one piece of content every month.

Content that showcases your expertise and the results your company can produce and can be in the form of articles, podcasts, TikToks, webinars, ebooks, etc. It doesn't really matter what kind of format you produce, as long as you stick with the process of publishing content.

This helps the people who booked calls to show up to the call better prepared.

There are also those prospects who haven't booked a call yet, but are looking around on your website or social media profiles and want to figure out a few things more about your business and your expertise before they schedule a call.

By openly sharing your expertise and putting your knowledge and your brand out there, you're significantly increasing the chances of a positive response.

Use these cold email boosters in line with good copy and even better targeting – and you'll be a cold email master in no time.

At the end of the day, these elements can help distinguish a cold email rookie from an expert. You don't want to be perceived as a rookie, right?

So, before launching your next campaign, put in place at least two or three of the activities from this chapter, and you'll start noticing an increase in calls booked and your overall conversion rate.

Chapter 29

Hiring an Outbound Team

Something I realized firsthand a few months after launching my first Cold Email campaigns, is that it's a full-time job, and not just one for one person.

What are the key roles you need to hire for, and why do you need to build a team that can run outbound sales campaigns in-house? Or, if you're looking to outsource the service what should you keep in mind?

Here are the three key roles you need to hire for:

1. Outbound Strategist
2. Lead Generation Expert
3. Campaign Manager

Outbound Sales Strategist

An important role that covers the following elements:

- Defining the niches to go after for each product or service you offer
- Building the Ideal Customer Profiles and targeting for each niche
- Brainstorming different targeting approaches to reach the right prospects
- Setting the goals and KPIs for the campaign, including how many prospects to reach out to every day/week/month, what are the expected results, how many email accounts
- Creating the main email flows that you're going to run
- Campaign optimization based on the results from each niche

Lead Generation Expert

The person researching the prospects and building lists. Their responsibilities can range from simple data entry and following a very detailed process, to doing data scraping, combining data from multiple sources, and building custom lead generation workflows.

When you're just starting out, especially if you're hiring in-house, and depending on your tech skills, it's more likely that you'll lean towards the first type of Lead Generation Expert. Generating prospect lists in a more manual and less scalable way.

As your experience running campaigns grows, you'll want to automate things as much as possible so you can scale.

Campaign Manager

Finally, we have the individual who creates and manages the campaigns using the campaign plan and the email copy from the Campaign Strategist. Then after the campaigns are live, the Campaign Manager follows up with prospects who respond using specific sales scripts and manages campaign reporting.

Some people like to have an appointment setter or BDR as a separate role. However, a good campaign manager will be able to manage your entire campaign process – at least in its early stages.

You can obviously outsource most parts of these roles, provided you have a clear process and training materials in place.

There are professionals from many different parts of the world with really solid sales and outbound skills. If you want to outsource part of the work, especially list building and campaign management, you can also look into other regions for qualified candidates.

Keep campaign strategy close to home as it's key to your campaign success. I would recommend being involved in the process personally or assigning it to an Outbound Sales expert proficient in your targeted industries.

Hiring a Cold Email Team

When hiring people for these roles, it's always important to send them an assignment to work on before you extend them an offer.

The recruitment process starts by writing a job description and publishing your job post. Besides including the role on your website, make sure to post it on platforms like LinkedIn, as well as on freelance websites like Upwork and Freelancer.com.

Each role needs to outline the responsibilities, as well as the success KPIs very clearly. These are performance sales positions, so it's important that everyone on the team knows which part of the Cold Email system they are contributing towards.

After people apply for the role, select 5 - 10 candidates for every position, and send them a small task to perform, related to that role. Here are some task ideas:

- **Lead Generation Expert:** build a list of prospects and create an Audience Research report for a specific ICP.
- **Campaign Manager:** build a campaign plan and assign email accounts to specific niches
- **Outbound Sales Strategist:** create a campaign strategy

You can work with freelancers on a few campaigns initially. Then, if you're happy with their work, get them on board as members of your team after 3-4 weeks.

Having full-time employees, when you're able to afford it, means achieving better results. Simply because your team is able to dedicate more of their time and their attention to making your campaigns successful.

Working as an Outbound Sales Consultant

You can still do most of the Cold Email work as a one-person team by structuring your day properly. Just because you can outsource the work to other people, it doesn't mean you have to.

Here's what the ideal day of an outbound sales consultant can look like:

- **Morning:** build prospect lists and engage on social media
- **Noon:** follow-up with existing prospects
- **Afternoon:** conduct sales calls
- **Evening:** review campaign performance and plan the next day

At the beginning of the day, spend one hour interacting with prospects and potential clients on social platforms like LinkedIn, Facebook, and Twitter. Add 10-20 prospects to your list, including details like their email address, phone number, LinkedIn profile, and company details.

Write personalized intros for prospects you add, then upload these with your list of prospects to your outreach tool.

Next, go through your email and social inboxes, respond to the prospects already engaged with your campaigns, and follow up on your sales calls and activities – including tasks like sending over your sales deck, creating a proposal for a new deal, etc.

Lastly, towards the end of your day, review your campaign performance, and activity levels, and ensure that you're within your goals and following your campaign plan.

When it comes to sales calls, you'll need to dedicate specific slots for them during your day. Your #1 priority should be to align with your ideal customers' work hours as much as possible for those calls.

The other key is selecting which hours of the day you want to be engaging with other people and feel the most communicative.

It's not important whether that's at the beginning of your day or the end of your day. As long as it actually fits your schedule and your energy levels. You want to be on the sales calls with maximum energy levels and a positive attitude.

Picture your ideal workday. For me, it's a late afternoon filled with sales calls, leaving the morning open for creativity and focus.

What about you? Are you a morning sales bird or an evening sales owl? If you don't know, well, it's experiment time! Shuffle your sales calls around and see what clicks. Build your perfect workday - it's in your hands.

As a bonus, you can download job descriptions for hiring your rockstar Outbound Sales team, including qualification questions for each role, by visiting coldemailsecrets.co/resources

Chapter 30

Building Businesses With Cold Email

T his is probably one of the *most important* chapters for achieving success with Cold Email. It covers the models you need to build your business with Cold Email.

Before establishing a new marketing and sales channel, it's important to define what you want to achieve from each channel.

If you don't have goals, you don't have a compass. And if you don't have a compass, you might achieve a lot of small wins, but not necessarily towards the direction that your business needs to go. Your strategy ends up failing after a few months. And you give up on cold email or any other channel you're trying.

So the first step is starting with the goal. And the goal should always be business growth, on any channel you're leveraging. Same with cold email, regardless if you use it to grow your business, or your clients' businesses.

What do these goals look like?

You should aim for 8-10% revenue growth from the previous operating period of your business. Whether that's a year or quarter.

How do you do that? Well, if you need one new client to get to 10% growth or 20% growth, you should aim to get that one new client. Once you have that number, the rest of the work becomes much easier.

There are three levels of operation when running outbound sales campaigns. Here's the breakdown of each level, including the kind of results you should be aiming for with each level:

Level 1: Starter

This is where you start if you haven't run Outbound Sales before. On this level, you're aiming to get between 2-3 sales every month from Cold Email. This is what the breakdown looks like:

- Prospects Engaged: 3,000
- Positive Replies: 10-20
- Calls Booked: 5-15
- Sales: 2-3

You reach out to about 3,000 prospects a month, sending 3-4 emails per prospect. You get about 10-20 positive replies per month.

From those prospects that responded, you book between 5-15 sales calls every month. And then, depending on your close rate, you close 2-3 deals every month.

To be successful on the Starter level, you need at least 3 email accounts and one domain to send those emails from. Ideally, that's not your main domain.

The activities on the Starter Level are also something you can do solo – the volume of leads is completely manageable. Alternatively, you can hire one individual who's proficient in sales outreach and outsource the campaigns.

Leveraging the right Cold Email tools, implementing the Cold Email automations we walked through, and using the specific processes from this book, should be a walk in the park.

Level 2: Growth

On this level, you want to reach out to more prospects and close more sales every month.

The typical question I get at this point, is *why not start my campaigns from level two or level three altogether, even if I haven't done this before?*

The answer is really simple. And it's the same as running Facebook ads or any other type of performance marketing campaign.

If you wake up one day and decide to spend $10,000 on Facebook ads without ever having run ads, it's going to be a waste of your budget.

The reason is you don't have the foundations in place for your budget to be spent well. You don't know if you're targeting the right audience. You haven't optimized your copy or your landing page against that audience. And you don't know what your baseline results look like. Your funnel is not optimized for conversions.

Realistically speaking, you can't really know what an optimized funnel looks like unless you've already run campaigns for that audience.

That's why it's best to start running your ads or start sending cold emails at a smaller volume. Therefore, when you're just starting out with your campaigns, it's always level one. The Starter level.

Once you've started to hit the KPIs from the **Starter level** consistently, getting two to three sales a month, you can move to the Growth level. Because by that point, your Cold Email funnel will have gone through enough iterations to be able to handle the volume and scale, without underperforming.

Level two is where things start getting more serious. It's when you need to build a team and a solid Outreach system, and probably create a training around your system so that you can hire more people.

Here's what the Growth level includes:

- Prospects Engaged: 5,000
- Positive Replies: 20-50
- Calls Booked: 10-30
- Sales: 2-3

You reach out to 5,000 prospects per month, and get between 20-50 positive responses. Once again, you're probably starting from the lower end of that, getting between 20-30 positive replies initially. You want to continue optimizing your campaigns and your messaging until you reach all the way to 50 positive replies per month.

Out of the 50 replies, you can get between 10 - 30 calls booked, and then generate five sales from those calls.

Now, if you're sending 5,000+ emails a month, you need at least seven email accounts to make that happen. And if you need seven email accounts, you're no longer good with just one additional domain. You need a second one.

You have three emails on one domain on the **Starter level**. At this stage, you need to buy a new domain and create three to four email accounts on that new domain.

That way, you're limiting your risks. Even if one of your email accounts gets marked as spam, you can set it aside for one to two weeks, until it's warmed up and healthy again, to start being used on campaigns.

The **Growth level** is where things get serious, and it's the next step from the Starter level. If you've done really well, and you're getting about 35 - 40 calls a month booked on this level, you can move to the next level.

Level 3: Scale

This is excellent when scaling to new geographies or when you already know quite well what messaging works for an audience, and want to introduce a supplementary product or service.

You've already validated both the message as well as the audience, so it's only a matter of reaching more people with your message.

This is why expanding the new geographies is probably the best use case for this level. It could also be because you hired more salespeople, opened up an office in a different country, or just decided to expand your market.

Here's what level three includes:

- Prospects Engaged: 8,000 - 10,000
- Positive Replies: 40-100
- Calls Booked: 20-60
- Sales: 10

You reach out to 10,000 prospects every month, get between 40 and 100 positive replies, and 40-60 calls booked. As a result of that, you can expect to sign 10 or more clients every month using this setup.

Now, to be able to send up to 10,000 emails a month, you'll need at least 13 email accounts and five domains. Make sure you divide the number of emails per domain equally, so you don't take any big risks by having most of your email accounts on one domain.

The cost of infrastructure has increased at this stage because even at $39 a month for each of the accounts, you'll have a flat cost of $500+ plus every month just for cold email tools.

This starts becoming a big investment for you to have the team, processes, and bandwidth to generate 10,000 prospects every month, so I would not recommend that someone launches their outreach campaigns expecting to reach out to that many prospects.

If you just start your campaigns and expect to be making 10 sales a month, sending 10,000+ emails, you're gonna find yourself in trouble because you'll end up spamming people.

Spam is when your message hasn't had time to mature for every niche you're reaching out to, and thus feels blunt and almost irrelevant to your prospects.

This eventually means your accounts are marked as spam, and your domains can get blacklisted quite easily.

The best strategy is to start from level one and then upgrade your campaigns to the next level every four months, after hitting the Gold KPIs on every level. Having open rates above 60%, CTR above 6%, and reply rate above 5%.

Campaign Strategies

Another tip that has to do with campaign volumes is running a lot of small campaigns with 100-1,000 prospects on each campaign with a personalized copy for each of the campaigns is much, much better than running a few bigger campaigns.

For example, if your goal is to send 3,000 emails per month, it's best to have 4-5 campaigns, targeting slightly different audiences with variations of your message specific to each segment.

That allows you to become even more personal with your copy, and that increases the chances you'll get a positive response from your prospects. Your click-through rate would increase, and you'd get more meetings booked at the end of the day.

It's important to emphasize, at this point, that the above metrics and KPIs represent averages from multiple industries and deal sizes. From B2B SaaS companies all the way to companies pushing enterprise deals. They act as a minimum benchmark.

Meaning that if you get better results with your campaigns, tap yourself in the back and keep doing what you're doing. If not, keep optimizing your message, and stick to lower outreach volumes till you've figured out the combination of audience and message that works.

Outsourcing Tips

When it comes to prospecting and list building, you should always research the first 100 prospects yourself. Both as a business owner and as a consultant working with SDRs. This allows you to really dig deep into the target audience.

After you have successfully researched and then populated a sheet with hundred prospects, you will have a crystal clear idea about who these people are, what communities they hang out in, what their interests are, what their goals are, what their roles in the company look like, what are their fears, what are their strengths, and what peaks their curiosity.

Then, you can hire in SDR, either part-time or full-time, to do the list-building and personalization of the message at scale.

In terms of volumes, a human can research and personalize between 70-100 emails a day. Always depending, always on the complexity of the ICP. If you need them to review multiple data points, like if the company is running ads, if the website looks out of touch, etc., they would generate fewer prospects every day, though 70-100 prospects per day are the goal.

Prospect Volumes

What about the number of prospects to target from every company you're reaching out to? The answer is that this depends on the size of the company.

If it's an SMB, a small and midsize business, you can add 1-2 people to your prospect list from companies with less than 20 employees. All the way to 5-6 people for companies that have 20-50 employees, provided you can find people with relevant job titles to what you're looking for.

The secret for this is you don't want to be messaging more than one person from each company at the same time. If two people from the same company, or the same department, with similar roles, receive the same message, you're really likely to be perceived as a spammer, or someone running mass cold email campaigns, which puts people off.

You don't wanna do that. You wanna be messaging one single individual at each time. If that individual doesn't respond or unsubscribe from your campaigns two weeks after the campaign is done for that prospect, your campaign manager should add one more person from that company to the campaigns. Until you get a response from that company, positive or negative.

That's why, on a research level, it's really important to be mapping out the list of companies that you're gonna be reaching out to within the next month, so it's really clear which prospects you'll be reaching out to with every campaign.

Niche Targeting

The last part of the equation is you want to be targeting two to three niches per month. By niches, I mean targeting audiences with a significant variation in terms of their traits.

That could be prospects coming from different sub-niches or different data sources. For example, targeting prospects that engage with a specific influencer in your niche vs. prospects that have joined a community or prospects you can find through sales intent tools.

The reason for that is when you're doing Cold Email, at the early stages, it's not a numbers game, it's a quality game. Meaning you want to make sure that your message resonates with people, and that they're actually in the market for a solution like the one you're promoting.

If you try to go after too many niches at the same time or target too many people at the same time, you're gonna end up creating really bad experiences for many people. You don't wanna be creating bad PR at large, and creating the perception that your company is spamming the market.

So these are, in a nutshell, the process behind running successful cold email campaigns. The pieces of the puzzle you need to keep in mind in order to keep your accounts healthy, protect your company's reputation, and boost your chances of success with cold email.

Chapter 31

Establishing Channel Model Fit

There is a specific spectrum of Average Revenue Per User (ARPU) and Customer Acquisition Cost (CAC) where cold email is the most efficient channel for bringing both sales and awareness to your business.

The average revenue per user (or per account in the case of selling services) determines how much you can afford to spend to acquire customers – and your customer acquisition cost. Based on these two metrics, some pricing models just aren't built for specific channels.

Cold email works best if you're making above $10,000 a year for every customer, account, or project you sell. This is what we typically call a high-ticket item or sale.

The question I frequently get is, *'Can cold email work for low-ticket products?'* or *'Can I actually message a high number of individuals to get them to buy my coaching product, my SaaS, or my software?'*

When selling lower-ticket digital or physical products, Cold Email can still be a valuable weapon. The best use for cold email is in establishing high-value relationships. That's the most basic principle of Cold Email.

Using that definition, you can still absolutely use Cold Email to sell low-ticket products, but you would use it in a different way. You wouldn't go after your end customers.

You would instead use it to build partnerships with companies that have access to the audience or the network to sell your product. Companies that could sell your product as a complementary product to theirs or as an upsell to their product. And companies or influencers with complimentary products and services that you could do co-marketing activities.

Let's say you have built a Cold Email software with a unique new feature that costs $39/month per seat. Why not reach out to the top 100 outbound sales agencies, who are already using a cold email tool, and try to get them to switch to your software?

You would instantly gain 10, 50, or 100 new client accounts for every agency you onboard. That would generate a lot more word of mouth and would have a much more significant impact on your bottom line than messaging 100k people at once, ending up spamming people, and not converting that many people as users.

If you know there are specific groups of people that are really likely to be in need of your service or your product and make heavy use of it, it's definitely a good idea to reach out to them. This category usually includes agencies, power users, targeted communities of business professionals, and influencers in your industry.

You can also use Cold Email for multiple other reasons, even if you're not selling high-ticket products or services that warrant building an outbound team.

Whether your goal is to secure meetings with potential investors for your next funding round, build backlinks to your content, or get to speak at conferences, cold email can be a powerful weapon.

I know about it firsthand, as twice a year I would have to recruit 100+ world-class Marketing speakers for Ad World. Wouldn't have made it without my Personalization Formula and a lot of automation.

In the next chapter, we'll dive deeper into more of these use cases.

Chapter 32

Additional Use Cases

As we've outlined, cold email can do a lot more than help you close sales deals. There's a multitude of use cases for it, and my goal is to help you leverage it to its full extent. Here are some of them:

- Recruiting top talent
- Establishing Partnerships
- Getting featured on podcasts
- Attracting guests to your podcast
- Pitching to VCs and Angel Investors

Let's go through them one by one, including cold email templates you can use for each case.

Recruiting Top Talent

The best professionals out there are either building their own businesses or working for other businesses. The chances that they will apply to your job post exist but are not in your favor.

If you are dead serious about making a specific outcome happen, you wouldn't just make a wish, publish a job post, and hope you somehow attract the perfect candidate. You want to take matters into your own hands.

So why not use Cold Email to reach out to candidates that already have the experience and skills you're looking for, and get them excited to work with you?

This can be used whether you run a talent placement agency, sourcing talent on behalf of your clients, whether you're an in-house HR manager that wants to attract more qualified candidates, or you're a solo founder looking to get your first employee.

You don't want to rely solely on the people who apply to your job position or have to spend a ton of money and time on ads. Your goal is to attract the best talent in the market. Cold Email can be the silver bullet that makes this happen.

Here is a template you can use:

Subject: *{{UniversityName}} + {{CurrentCompany}} intro*

Hey {{firstName}}, great to connect! CEO of {{Company}} here.

I just finished reading your post on {{topic}}.

It's really well-written, and I'm a huge fan of {{topic}} as well.

We just announced our partnership with {{Partner}} and are scaling up our team.

Are you free for a 10min chat, and if so, how's tomorrow at 1 pm?

Bill

Here's one more template:

Hey {{firstName}},

It's Bill from {{Company}}.

We're looking for a sales manager and your profile came high on LinkedIn Search as an expert on the topic.

I was wondering if you could give me 5 mins of your time on how you'd build out our sales team.

Best, Bill

Establishing Partnerships

Partnerships allow you to grow by leveraging people who have larger audiences, more leverage, or more connections and contacts than you in the industry you're looking to sell to.

It's an incredible channel that people tend to overlook when trying to sell their products and services. Building partnerships with companies that sell similar but not competitive products to yours. With solution providers and people who have access to audiences, you can help. It can make a big difference to your growth.

A software company called Zapier grew to $140 million in ARR with a valuation of $5 billion by building and executing a partnerships playbook. They dedicated time and resources to establishing ties and integrations with other software businesses.

It paid out big-time, and there are countless more examples of the same success – many food delivery apps, like Uber Eats, Wolt, Delivery Hero, and Deliveroo, rely on outreach strategies to attract restaurants to their platform.

Here's a template for that:

Subject: *{{CompanyName}} x {{OurCompany}} idea*

Hey {{firstName}},

My name is Bill, I run Notion's partnerships team, and we work with companies like Google, ClickUp, Hubspot, etc.

I saw you just launched the Speechify iOS app, and I wanted to explore what a partnership looks like. We have more than 20 million users today, 85% of whom create and share readable content every week.

We have an idea for a collaboration that could benefit our and your existing customers. If you're interested, we'd love to talk next steps with your team.

Best, Bill

Getting Featured on Podcasts

The next use case for cold email is what I call authority building, and it's a really powerful activity. It's using cold email to get featured on podcasts and publications. This gives your business and personal brand a lot of exposure and perceived authority from the press mention.

Use tools like Roxhill, Muckrack, and SparkToro to find potential journalists and podcasts for features – pitch your story and leverage their audience to sell your products more effectively.

Here's a template you can use:

__Subject:__ {{PastPodcastGuest}} on {{Podcast}} was 🔥

Hey {{firstName}},

I've listened to a few episodes of {{Podcast}} and I really loved your work!

{{Icebreaker}}

After listening to the podcast, I think your audience would love to hear from {{teamMember}}, our {{Position}} at {{OurCompany}}. {{teamMember}} can share some in-depth, actionable insights about {{topic}}, plus how we've grown from $0 to 2M ARR in 2 years, bootstrapped.

{{Here's}} their LinkedIn profile for some reference.

And, of course, we'll have our audience tune in from:
- *The biggest advertising community (23K+ members)*
- *Social media profiles (120K+ followers combined)*
- *Our newsletter of 40K subscribers*

• *An active audience of Marketing, Sales, and Growth professionals*

Anyways, I'd love to hear your ideas! What do you say?

Cheers, Bill

Attracting Guests to Your Podcast

Building a podcast and securing guests can have multiple benefits – both for your business and personally. It helps you build content for your nurturing campaigns and expand your network with interesting people you wouldn't have access to otherwise.

Let's say there's an Instagram influencer you admire. Instead of pitching them to join you for a call, you can invite them to your podcast and promise to advertise it using paid ads to bring them more followers.

They'll love you for it, you'll get the authority of talking to them and be able to tap into their audience.

This strategy works really well for getting new clients as well. Invite them on your podcast to share their thoughts, problems, and solutions. it will be a very natural transition to a sales call if you have a good solution to recommend.

So start inviting people that you might be friends with, people from within your industry, and people you respect, and get them to share their knowledge and expertise on your podcast.

Here's a template for you:

Subject: {{firstName}} podcast invite

Hey {{firstName}},

Bill here from SalesCaptain.

I've been following your work for a while now. I really like your writing style. I especially enjoyed when you said {{Quote}}.

Since we're both in the business of creating content around {{Topic}}, I thought it would be nice to connect.

More than that, I'd like to invite you as a guest on my podcast, {{PodcastName}}. If you're interested, I'd love to discuss your ideas around {{Topic}} further.

Let me know what you think.

Talk soon, Bill

Networking With Anyone

When visiting a new city or just want to expand your network, make some time to meet a few interesting people you wouldn't otherwise have access to.

Provide some context but keep it to the point. Be flexible with the time slots you offer. If they're in your industry, mention a conference or event you can attend together. Be creative with the CTA; inviting them for a workout session at the gym or a quick run might be more fun than just 'grabbing coffee.'

Subject: in {{City}} – let's meet!

Hey {{firstName}}, I'm in {{City}} next week for {{Reason}}! (coming from {{YourCity}} ✈)

Would love to hear more from you about {{Company}}, share how we've evolved over the past four years, and see if there's anything we can do together.

I'll be staying near St. Paul's Cathedral! Happy to meet for coffee around there in the afternoon from Monday to Wednesday.

Let me know what time is convenient!

Pitching to VCs and Angel Investors

VCs get bombarded with cold emails every day. Depending on their visibility and reputation, a particular VC may get 10 - 100 cold emails daily.

The secret to cutting through the noise is getting a referral from another VC or a portfolio founder of a specific angel investor.

Here's what that would look like

Subject: *Face recognition AI startup with 32k MRR - raising 3M*

Hi {{firstName}},

I've recently spoken to X from Y, who is in your portfolio, and they said amazing things about you. In particular, how helpful you were in helping them establish a scalable GTM strategy for the US market in 2023.

I'm one of the co-founders of {{Company}}. We are currently entering the US market as well, having achieved PMF in Canada and Brazil, growing at 23% MoM for the last 12 months.

Here's a 60 seconds video where our clients share how they benefit from our solution. We are now at $Y MRR, aiming to raise $XX within the next {{Time Period}} to reach $YYY MRR within the next {{Time Period}}.

I would love to have a chat and present you with our vision of becoming the {{vision}}.

Ps. The growth {{Company in their portfolio}} had in Q2 is just crazy.

Best, Bill

Chapter 33

Next Steps

W e've almost reached the end of our journey together into the world of Cold Email. A world that has completely changed my life and can do the same to yours.

What started as a one-off campaign for a client turned into a $1M business, a Go-to-Market agency, the world's largest Marketing lineup, and the book you have in your hands.

The final level of building a successful business is mastering the art of connecting with people you don't know to achieve greater things together. And that starts with one simple, well-crafted email.

You now have a better overview of the process and systems for building successful Cold Email campaigns than most people out there.

This is an incredible power that you can use to thrive both in your personal as well as your professional life. Just remember, you're not a spammer, so try not to act like one.

Remove any guilt associated with Cold Email, and focus on providing value and building genuine relationships. You'll be amazed by what's possible when you set your mind to it. I know I certainly am.

Here's what you can do next:

- Download all the assets and resources of the book at coldemailsecrets.co/resources
- Making below $10k MRR: get early access to the Outbound Sales course at coldemailsecrets.co/course
- Making above $10k MRR: get early access to the Outbound Sales course for your team, or apply for an outbound strategy session to see if cold email can fit your growth stage
- Send this book to someone you think needs to hear this so they can get unstuck and continue growing their business

If you're looking for help with your cold email strategy and systems, don't hesitate to reach out. I'm always happy to help.

Onwards and upwards, my friend!

Best regards, Bill